BACK IN THE DAY

By

Aaron Briese

Copyright Year: 2007
Copyright Notice: by Aaron Briese. All rights reserved.

Results in this copyright notice:

© 2007 by Aaron Briese. All rights reserved.
ISBN 978-0-6151-4381-1

CHAPTER 1
CAN'T START FROM THE BEGINNING

Today I told another little story about my past to my co-workers, and for the twenty-first time in my life, someone has suggested that I write a book. After telling a small part of the whole fucked up picture, they all seemed shocked that someone's life can be so convoluted, yet manage to end up on the correct path in life. After all the things I've seen and done, some people find it hard to believe I survived it at all. But honestly, there were a few times there that I almost didn't. I'm getting ahead of myself here. I probably need to go back a ways and find some spot to jump in and begin telling my story.

It's not easy deciding where to begin, but at least I know where not to begin. My childhood seems to be wrapped in a blanket of fog. At the ripe old age of thirty-six, I can't seem to remember any of my childhood. Maybe I'm blocking it out, or maybe it just didn't have any significant moments for me to remember. I grew up in what I call a slightly abusive household. I can't say that I got my ass beat every day, but I do remember some days that my punishment didn't seem to fit my crime. But that's how it seems to always work out for me. So my childhood is a blur. Even when I talk to friends from the past and my family, they remember a lot more of my childhood than I do. I just stay quiet, nod my head, and absorb my younger trials and tribulations, without ever really remembering those things happening to me. Sometimes I even wonder if we're talking about the same person. So I think I'd need to do a little more investigating into my childhood before that story can be unfolded and laid out for everyone to see. That's OK though because picking up the story from when I left home will still fill a whole book. It won't be a rated G or PG story, but it definitely will have its moments, and I think that if I write it all down on paper, I won't have to worry about losing it in that fog that grows over time.

So this story will begin by describing a few of the hooligans I considered friends in high school. First off, all through junior high and high school, I was that small kid who got picked on and beat up each day. When I woke up, if there wasn't any way to avoid going to school, I would have to choose the bus or walking.

Walking from my house to school took anywhere from forty-five minutes to an hour and a half, depending on which direction I went. Of course, the forty-five minute path had more bullies, and went through a worse neighborhood, and was just all around dangerous. But even that was better than the school bus; I really hated the school bus because once you got on it, you were trapped on it until you got to school. The time spent on the bus seemed to go by in slow motion. The faster I wanted it to go by, and the ride to end, the longer it felt like it took.

From the very beginning, you learn that a bus driver is just someone hired by the school to pick kids up and take them from home to school and home again. They don't police the bus and they don't really care what goes on. There was always smoking in the back of the bus, but the bus driver never said anything about it. Whatever else went on during the bus ride was also overlooked.

I had things thrown at me by kids on the bus, all kinds of things. I didn't want to know what it might be. They also liked to pour stuff down the backs of the seats. The net result was that many times I ended up spending the day in school with a wet, sticky, or foul smelling shirt and pants, an unfortunate result of the soda or whatever had been poured on the seat.

Some days nothing at all happened. But that false sense of security didn't last very long and when the tormenting started up again it seemed even worse. Getting gum in your hair can really put a damper on your day as well. So by 9th or 10th grade, it was easier to walk to school. Riding the school bus was a lot shorter in real-time but with the problems I had to put up with for that luxury, the long walk was much less stressful.

So, I started walking to school. That was a nice break from the turmoil on the bus and at school. But it was short lived, because my path to school led right through a neighborhood of the lower income families. That's where most of the bullies originated in my neck of the woods. But it made it easier to find them later on in the future; you'll understand how that fits in later on in the story. So after walking to school for a couple weeks, some of the larger and not always older kids started to take notice of me. This was not a good thing. They always approached me in packs of four or more but it wasn't like they needed the backup. They were all pretty big to me, so one or two could have easily done the job, but they always traveled in these groups, mainly being together just to egg each other on to commit these dastardly deeds.

There were always a few loudmouths in the group, talking a lot of shit and asking questions that no matter how I answered, it was the wrong answer. I remember running a lot and getting caught a lot. The ass beating was the least of my concerns; I've taken plenty of those in my life from people a lot larger than some teenage bullies. It was the fear that I hated the most, being scared just walking up the street, wondering if they would be waiting in the shadows that day. My eyes constantly scanned the path ahead of me, looking for any possible trouble, and any means of egress in case I found myself in another tough bind. But the walk to and from school wasn't the only time I got picked on and tortured. It was just one of the only places where I had nowhere to run and no one was going to help me. School wasn't much better but at least I didn't feel that constant fear. Sure, there was also before school, during school, and after school, but most of those situations could be controlled in one way or another. It's easy to not be at the school for any reason before or after school. No after school activities because it was just easier to not go at all than to take a chance that one or more of the asshole bullies would be there. During school wasn't as bad; there always were teachers and principals walking around and I could always just head over toward one of them if trouble arouse.

It really sucked to be a late bloomer, as my parents liked to call it. I'm over six feet tall now and weigh nearly two hundred pounds, but in junior and senior high, I was much, much smaller. Being one of the smartest kids in the class just added to the ammo for the bullies. Then, in my sophomore year I had what I would call my first epiphany. I came to a sudden realization. It's amazing what fear every single day for four years can do to your thinking process. I decided that I couldn't handle this for much longer. I missed a lot of school, pretending to be sick, or just walking somewhere else. As long as I kept getting A's on all my tests and learned how to forge my parent's signature, the school didn't really care that I wasn't there thirty percent of the time. But with the home life I had, staying at home could be like walking a minefield as well.

What's really sad is how lately I've been seeing a growing trend of picked on, terrified kids who feel that they have to resort to bringing a gun to school because they feel like their backs are against the wall. I in no way support what they've done or how they felt they needed to stop feeling that fear, but I can completely understand exactly where their heads were at. I understand how hard it is to live everyday feeling like you are all alone, except for maybe a handful of friends who are in the same boat as you, being picked on every day, by people who ten years down the road won't even remember you let alone what they did to you or how it affected you for the rest of your life.

I read the book "Carrie" by Stephen King as well as watched the movie. In it, a girl gets invited to a dance as a practical joke, just to torment her for laughs. I was always worried something terrible like that would happen to me at the school dances, but I didn't really have to concern myself, since I never went to a dance unless I went alone. The one girl I really liked back then wasn't allowed to see me but we hung out on the sly for a while and talked on the telephone. But it was just too difficult to attempt to hide it so we just quit talking.

It's sad when I think back about it and all a person can do is wonder, "What if?" But, that is in the past and although we never married and lived happily ever after, I have talked to her, just to let her know what happened to me. After all of these years, I was finally able to tell her how special she was to me, what she meant to me and still means to me to this day.

But the last time I saw her face to face, I felt as if I were intruding on her life, rather interrupting her life, when things were going along fine for her. I felt like I might have been upsetting her world and my intentions were not that.

It wasn't so much one specific incident, but years of never ending instances that built up. I started to hate school, not the learning aspect of it but the social contact. In between classes was when the bullies grouped up and harassed people. It was their entertainment after an hour in a boring class. It was too bad that I had to be their entertainment.

If you push a kid too far, make him feel like a trapped animal with no way out, eventually that kid is going to have some sort of breakdown. For me it was the choice of not going to school half of the time. Avoidance seemed my best option. I went in mainly on test days and got A's on all of my tests. On the days I missed, I practiced my forgery skills on parent absent and permission slips. The school didn't seem to care if I was present or not, which was perfectly fine by me.

Other kids didn't make that choice. Maybe their parents made them go to school or the school demanded that the child be present? So instead, they had to endure it day after day. You never knew when something might happen, so you had to be scared and worried the entire day. You had a constant knot in your stomach and the hairs on the back of your neck were all prickly every time that you had to venture out into the halls between classes. Sometimes nothing at all happened, but you couldn't ever let your guard down because of the times that something did. You remember those for a while. With that to look forward to each and every day, it becomes clearer exactly what pushes a kid to bring a gun to school. I can understand what they were going through, before it all went too far.

For a couple of weeks, I carried a big buck knife in my school bag, thinking that it might help, but I was too scared to ever pull it on someone, even if he was kicking my ass at the time. And after two or three weeks I managed to cut myself with it screwing around with it in my bag, so I quit carrying it. The scariest part of the whole situation was that if I would have had access to a gun, I honestly think I would have brought it to school. I might not have used it, but I definitely would have pulled it, just to show some of these people a small bit of the fear I'd been feeling for the past four years. It wouldn't have been a sudden, rash decision, but the fear I was experiencing would have pushed me to it. You feel like there's nothing else you can do, and you want to fight back, but you don't know how. They try to blame this on the TV and the kid's parents but that's not where the onus of blame should fall. You can't even blame it on the

school; it's just the largest gathering place of assholes and bullies.
The school can't be held responsible, unless they knew it was going to happen and did nothing to stop it, which no school would ever do or want to happen. You can't really point fingers at any one specific person or group, but when it all adds up, you get a little powder keg in the shape of a terrified teenager. A kid who feels he has no other alternative than to put an end to the fear he is suffering from. And I can tell you from experience that these kids wish they wouldn't have reacted this way, and in retrospect maybe there were other ways to remedy this constant fear, but at the time, it seemed the only way to stop it.

Now back to my epiphany. I had no access to large weapons, and my fear probably wouldn't have allowed me to do anything rash anyway, so I did what I felt was the next best thing. I made friends with a couple of the biggest and meanest guys around. I helped them with their homework, bent over backwards for them, and they took total advantage of that, but I had bodyguards now. I called them friends but that's what they really were. My daily life of getting picked on drastically decreased. It wasn't that they protected me per se, but when I was with them, nobody messed with me. When they weren't around, it was a different story, but at least I felt safe a lot more often. They would never fight a fight for me or anything like that, but just their mere presence kept the other assholes away for awhile. But these guys were bad news in their own right. They corrupted me as well as protected me. I started smoking, drinking, stealing, you name it; they were talking me into doing it. A lot of it I did because I didn't want to lose their 'friendship,' but some of it I did because it was a different kind of fear. This fear wasn't like the fear of torture. At times the rush of actually doing it, and reliving it with these 'friends' was exhilarating and slightly addictive. I never came up with the ideas, but I was always one of the first to actually go through with them. They thought it was because I had balls of stone, but it was actually fear driving me. I was afraid if I didn't, I'd lose my 'friends' and be back to the same situation I was in before. So needless to say, we did a lot of stupid shit.

It progressively got worse until in my senior year, when we were out 'car hopping' one night, or actually early morning. The night before, we went into a lot of parked cars next to an apartment complex, checking for unlocked cars, and rooting around in them for stupid shit like change and cigarettes and lighters. While we were in a couple of cars parked near each other, the owner of one of the cars came running out in his underwear, and he was huge. I've had a lot of practice in my childhood running for my life, so like a bullet I was gone. Everyone was running behind me but one of us got caught by the guy. He had no interest in calling the cops, he just wanted to pound on us, which he did to my 'friend' Todd. He broke Todd's arm, broke his nose, and gave him two black eyes. Todd was crying when we finally found him lying on the ground in a field.

Unbelievably, he was the lucky one.

The next night/morning while Todd was recuperating in the hospital, we were at it again, this time taking everything we found in these people's cars. We even went back and vandalized the three cars from the night before because we weren't sure which car belonged to the ape that kicked the crap out of Todd. Next we went behind a row of condos down the street and started checking those cars. That's when we found the wallet full of credit cards... and the loaded gun. It was one of those little 38 special handguns that held five or six shots. It was under the front seat of the car, and in the glove compartment was a box of bullets. Finding that in one car, and a wallet with money and credit cards in another, we felt like it was our lucky night.

My father is a very patient man. I guess he would have to be, to put up with a kid like me. I always seemed to find trouble, and he was always there to bail me out. With all of the serious pitfalls in life, he just seemed to roll with the punches. Now, as an adult, I learn more from him each and every day that I spend with him. He taught me the most important thing in life. He gave me part of his wonderful sense of humor and how important laughter is.

I don't really remember the exact circumstances, but he took me out to buy a car. We shopped around for used cars until we found this ugly burnt orange 1974 Toyota Corolla hatchback. It cost $500.00 and it ran good. The interior was torn up when I got it, so a roll of duct tape and a couple of seat covers later it was like new to me. It also was a 5-speed stick shift, but you learn how to drive a car with a clutch pretty quickly when you don't have a choice.

That little car could tell quite a few stories. I must have put 100,000 miles on it and only had to change the water pump. I even taught my best friend Eric to drive in it.

Although Eric was a couple of years younger than me, we saw everything on the same level. What I liked best about him was that I always felt like I could talk to him. Our lives were so similar that it was easy to become friends. We talked about everything and we still do to this day.

I think it was during my junior year of high school when Eric and I got into trouble for the last time together. In the past we had been getting into trouble with our parents for things like sneaking out after our parents were in bed, smoking and just stupid teenage boy stuff.

Eric's mother finally put her foot down and we weren't allowed to be friends any more. I didn't talk to him again for almost fifteen years.

Once we finally came in contact with one another again and started comparing notes on our lives, we saw some very amazing similarities. But in the end we both got our lives together and made something of ourselves. Eric is one of the most talented musicians I have ever met and I've met quite a few.

So Eric missed out on just about this entire story, but he did get to experience the 'Piece of Shit Car'. I say that in a very nice way though. That car was extremely dependable and a great place to sleep if I had had too much to drink or just didn't want to go home.

We all piled into my 'piece of shit' Toyota Corolla car and headed down Hemsath Road, nicknamed the seven hills of hell because you could get airborne if you drove down it fast enough. Many teenagers in my area either lost their lives or were permanently disabled on this road, but that only added to the mystique. It went way down into deserted, empty farmland, where no one could see or hear us. We went down there and got out the gun and bullets and took turns shooting it. Most of us had never fired a gun except a shotgun in our hunting class at school during a one-day field trip. (Yes we actually had a hunting and fishing class in Missouri back in the eighties. Scary, huh?) So we spent a few hours down there drinking beer and shooting this pistol at a tree. Then the beer and bullets ran out, both about the same time. I forget who, but one of us came up with the idea of trying to use these credit cards we found. Nobody had ever tried anything like this before so we came up with a pretty lame plan. We had some gas cards so we went to a gas station and filled the car up, went in the store and spent another fifty dollars on junk food and cigarettes. It worked like a charm, I signed for it and off we went. So now we have a foolproof scheme. By the end of the night we'd be rich. Unfortunately it didn't work out that way.

On the third or fourth gas station after that, where we had been spending close to a hundred dollars per station, I guess some red flag went up. It probably looked suspicious that this person's gas card is being used all over the Saint Louis, Saint Charles area, all in one night. At our final gas station, the attendant gave us what we wanted, but he seemed to be doing everything in slow motion. He ran the card four times, saying that the station had been having trouble with the card machine all night. Then, he could not find our brand of cigarettes, of which we wanted ten cartons. After a while he gave us everything we asked for, but when we walked out to the car, there were two police cars waiting for us, one parked in front of my car, the other parked behind. The police officers started asking all sorts of misleading questions, pretending not to be there for us, just happening to be passing by. But after ten minutes of questions and answers from us that would soon incriminate ourselves, the station attendant came out and told the cops that he was the one who called and that we were using a stolen credit card. The cops told him that they already knew about the card and were just giving us enough rope to hang ourselves with, which we did. We were now fucked, but we didn't quite understand just how fucked we were.

The officers handcuffed us and sat us on the ground while they went through the contents of my car. After four or five gas stations, we had a lot of stuff, so the process was slow and tedious, at least until they found the gun. Then all hell broke loose. The police officers got very angry that we didn't offer up the gun to begin with, but once one of the officers smelled the gun and saw that it was full of empty cartridges, they had a sinking suspicion that someone may have been shot by this weapon. They handcuffed all three of us, Kenny, Timmy, and me. They separated us and took us by ourselves to the station. They didn't want us cooking up some tall tale. When we got to the station, we were interviewed, and I was the last one they talked to. I told them the story about the car hopping and shooting the gun down on Hemsath Road. They said Kenny's story was a similar to mine but with him doing nothing, and Timmy's story was that he fell asleep in the back seat and has no idea where the gun came from.

While I was in the interrogation room, and almost finished with my story, a man entered the room in blue jeans and a T-shirt. He walked up to me and just blasted me with a right cross. I never even saw it coming. It knocked me out of my chair and onto the floor. All the uniformed officers just stood there and stared at me. I knew I had somehow truly fucked up because these police officers didn't seem like they were going to do anything about it but let it continue. He picked me up, threw me against the wall, and punched me again. But this wasn't some teenager or my mother hitting me; this guy was strong. I thought for sure I was going to black out if he continued much longer. I already couldn't catch my breath from being slammed against the wall and after a few punches to the stomach, I thought I was going to throw up on him, but I was afraid he'd kill me then. I couldn't understand how these cops could let some guy who wasn't even in uniform come in here and do this. Then he started talking and I realized just how deep into this shit I was.

He screamed into my face from less than two inches away from my nose, "Hey mother fucker, I'm an undercover narcotics agent for this department, I've been on this job for fifteen years, and I've killed MEN before, some with my bare hands. You don't know exactly how badly you've fucked up yet, but you will."

Then the ass whooping began again. He hit me a lot in the stomach and sides and chest. I didn't know it at the time, but it was so the damage he did wasn't as noticeable. No matter how much I cried and begged, this cop wouldn't let up. Finally he grabbed me by my shirt, pulled me up off the floor, and put his face

two inches away from mine again.
I had never seen someone as angry as that guy looked, but maybe my view was clouded by my fear and the constant pummeling.

With his face close enough to smell his breath, which was coming really fast, out of exhaustion from the beating or just blood lust, he said through gritted teeth, "You really fucked up, boy. That was my gun you stole. I had to get a call at my girlfriend's house from these friends of mine telling me that after running the serial number of the gun, it came back as belonging to me. They were nice enough to call me before reporting it to my captain. Going out to my car and finding my firearm gone was bad enough, but when I arrived down here and discovered that my firearm has been fired as well, I can't be held responsible for my actions. I'm going to ask you one time where all my bullets are, and if I find out you used this gun in a crime, or God forbid shot someone with my firearm, I will kill you with my bare hands. I want you to understand that so far there has been no paperwork started about you here. There is no proof that you are even here."

Now my fear had grown to the point of understanding that I might die there. And to prove the point, all the uniformed officers except one turned and walked out of the room. I was coming to that FUCKED realization. If I didn't start talking fast, this guy was really gonna hurt me, maybe permanently. That vision of Todd came back from just the day before, except now it seemed a lot longer than one day, Todd in the hospital after getting pounded.

So I said, "I SWEAR TO GOD YOUR GUN..."

"SHUT UP!!!!" he yelled back. "I told you I'm going to give you one chance to give me your story, but I haven't asked for it yet. I don't think you fully understand what consequences your answer may result in."

"Yes I do!!" I tried to slip in.

"SHUT THE FUCK UP!!! If you talk again, I'll bust you in the mouth. I've been very nice to your face so far. Let's keep it that way, OK?"

I nodded and said nothing.

At that point he made a lot of threats but I didn't really hear any of them. I already fully understood the trouble I was in. I guess he figured me to be like the hardened criminals he dealt with day in and day out, and not some kid who was already living in fear. I already knew what a bully was capable of, especially if he felt he could get away with it scot-free. And this guy was definitely a class one bully, but maybe that's what is required to be an undercover police officer. I've met my fair share of undercover NARCS over these thirty-six years, and they are all cut from the same cookie cutter mold. But they couldn't do what they have to do, day after day, unless they have a certain bullish personality. I've heard they have a high burnout rate and a high suicide rate, and if true, it's another sad situation with someone who feels he has no alternative but to do something drastic.

So after another of what seemed hours but I'm sure was just minutes, he threw me in my chair, showed me that he did indeed have his gun back, and said now's your chance to talk. So I did the bravest and only thing I could think of and just started bawling. I couldn't stop, the tears kept flowing, and my chest kept hitching so much I couldn't speak. You know, that was the last time I cried. Actually that's not true. That's the last time I cried until I was thirty-three. Now, I've discovered that at least I still can cry, but it takes my whole world ending for it to kick in.

When I finally got control of myself, the cop knew he had completely broken me, not knowing that I was pretty much broken already, long before meeting him. I told him everything and he just listened quietly, then got up and left with the uniformed officer. After a couple of hours the uniformed cop came back and said I was being charged and I had one phone call. I called my dad and like the old fashioned knight he is, he came rushing down to rescue me. He got me a private attorney and after a lot of court hearings and I'm sure a lot of money, I managed to get a deal that all charges would be dropped if I joined the Navy.

So as soon as I graduated, off to the Navy I went. I was actually excited about going in, and I was going in some high tech field that I thought I might enjoy. Unfortunately, I messed my knee up and was unceremoniously discharged on medical conditions. I got in trouble only one time there. It was for unauthorized smoking and my punishment was a 12 A.M. to 4 A.M. fire watch in a concrete and steel barracks that couldn't have burned down if it wanted to. I was in an unfamiliar area and the light was burned out. I didn't see the iron stairwell and fell down the steps, hyperextending my knee. It was bent almost 90 degrees the wrong way, and when the very large Navy nurse came on the scene, she proceeded to grab my thigh in one huge ham hock of a hand and my ankle in the other and snapped it back into place, breaking my kneecap in the process. I passed out and don't remember anything after that. Every time I tell a doctor this story, he just cringes and can't believe she did it that way, but I have the x-rays of my shattered knee to show her actual brutality. I spent two months in a wheelchair and another on crutches in a dorm full of guys who either lied and said they were gay or tried to kill themselves in order to get a discharge. The officers treated me just like I was one of the fakers they dealt with in this medical unit.

After three months of this I was taken to a room with some high-ranking officer who wanted to know if I wanted to be in the Navy. I said, yes I want to be here. This is the only place I can receive training in the field I want to specialize in, the nuclear field. I said I felt healthier and fitter than I've ever felt in my life. He excused himself from the room, and when he returned he had a chaplain with him. I guess he felt I needed someone on my side right about now. He then told me that I was to receive an honorable discharge under medical conditions. The doctors said that I had a 50% chance of having full mobility and probably wouldn't ever have more than 75% of my ability to use my knee. When he saw that I wasn't going to cry or go into a rampage, he asked the chaplain to leave. Then he got down to the nitty, gritty. He told me that either I can wait for this paperwork to be completed and I'd just have to continue living in this medical unit for another three to six months, or I could sign this EPTE paperwork and be released in about two and a half weeks. EPTE is entry prior to enlistment; pretty much saying that I had this problem before coming in and the Navy wasn't responsible. He knew what the Med unit was like, and I'm sure I wasn't the first person or the last that they pulled this on. He gave me a week to think about it, but I had made up my mind already, I just wanted out, and the sooner the better. I lost all respect for the Navy; I felt that they totally deserted me, so I just wanted to get away, to go back home and see what was there.

So back to Missouri I went, except I'd grown, gained a lot of weight, been physically training for months, and lost most of that fear I'd grown used to over the years. And my fear of physical pain was completely gone. I'd spent my childhood learning how to take a beating, and spent three months learning how to give one. So Missouri was a whole new ball game now.

CHAPTER 2
A BOLD NEW WORLD

So after messing my knee up, it was back to Missouri to see what kind of trouble I could get into. Of course that wasn't what I was thinking, but I probably should have been. Arriving back in Missouri was very anti-climactic, at least at first. Everyone and everything seemed exactly the same as it was before, but there was something new as well. It was me and my new attitude.

After only being back for a few days, and hobbling around everywhere on a cane, I wanted to see some of the few friends I had in high school. So I went to a place I knew some of them would be, just a parking lot that everyone use to hang out in. It was a weekend night so there were a lot of people there. I found a couple of people I knew and started talking to them, when out of nowhere one of the bullies in high school walked up. He made some crack about how I looked without hair and then asked me if I pussed out and faked my knee injury to get out of some tough place like the Navy. I never said a word; just let him finish, as I knew he eventually would. After the faked injury crack, he tried to kick my cane out from under me, and in what seemed like slow motion, I proceeded to beat the crap out of him with the cane, never taking more than one step, balanced on my one good knee. That fear was completely gone; all I felt was the rush of finally winning a battle, and like a little bit of justice was served. The only problem with the whole situation was how easy it was, and that just made me want to do it some more. I had a few moments in my life that I felt needed to be made up for. Some people call it revenge; I just called it sweet justice. There was a lot of baggage I was carrying for many years, and I was beginning to see an opportunity to relieve myself of some.

My next chance at watching and actually helping karma return to a few people was at the homecoming high school football game. I went there with two friends but I didn't go to see the game. I went looking for certain people. And lo and behold they were there. I ran into one guy right around halftime. Wayne or Dwayne, I can't remember. It's a small town, so news of my last fight traveled fast, especially since so many people saw it. He was one of the guys who lived between my house and my school and used to chase me and beat me up when he caught me. I even remembered the black eye he gave me once, although throughout the years I never once fought back. He walked up to me and said he'd heard about what happened in the parking lot and said that I must think I'm pretty tough with my cane. For the previous three days I had spent the whole day walking without my cane, to test my knee out and strengthen it up. So to his surprise, I turned to one of the guys I was with, and handed him my cane.

I asked, "Do you want to go outside the fence where there's no faculty?"

Without waiting for him to answer, I turned and walked off to the exit of the football field. When I got out there, Wayne wasn't that far behind, and he had a couple friends with him. I knew every one of them. My two friends looked a little nervous and weren't quite sure what I had just gotten them into. But they knew that I had a whole new attitude and they'd enjoyed the ride so far since my return from the Navy. As I walked out to the lot I realized that I wasn't scared. I wasn't scared at all, but I was full of a strong emotion. I was angry. I was pissed that these guys didn't see the change in me, I was pissed that I put up with their shit for so many years, and I was pissed that not enough people were going to see this. But I let it just build up.

There were four of them, three of us, and about five others that were just there to see a fight. So I knew this wasn't going to be fair from the beginning. As soon as the pack of us walked in between a row of buses, I spun around and hit Wayne square in the mouth as hard as I could, leaning all my weight on my good knee. That cop showed me that trick, and just like with me, he went down, and went down hard. Except unlike the cop, I tried to knock him out with the punch, the cop tried to just not split open my face too bad. I didn't knock him out, but I knocked his two front teeth out. One of his friends, who I remembered from my runs to and from school, stepped forward and started to say something, with his brow all scrunched up. So I hit him about four times until he turned and ran off. The other two guys didn't want to be there anymore and made themselves ghost. I know I probably shouldn't have felt good after that but with all these people, some I hardly knew, patting me on the back and telling me good job, it was hard to think straight. Now I had a chip on my shoulder. Without the fear, a lot of things started to come easier in life. But, I was going to discover that the anger has its setbacks as well.

After returning to Missouri, it didn't take long to discover that I no longer belonged there. So after I felt my knee was completely healed, I put a backpack on, walked up to highway 94, and stuck out my thumb. I made a decision that California was the place I wanted to be, but without striking oil, I had to resort to hitchhiking. I've done a lot of hitchhiking throughout my life. I'd never suggest that anyone try it, but every single one of my experiences was great, some better than others, but never a bad trip. I had hitchhiked throughout Saint Charles since I was twelve, but never anything like this. I had no idea what I was doing; I just knew I had to go.

I walked for a few hours, and some guy stopped in a brand new van with Michigan plates. I jumped in and he asked, " Where you going?"

I told him I was on my way to California and he said, "Me too! Jump in, my name's Mike and are you hungry?"

I didn't really have very much money in my pocket; I just figured to kind of work my way across country. I never planned to find a ride all the way there. I asked, " I don't really have much cash so can we eat somewhere cheap?"

Like he'd known me for years he said, "Oh don't worry about that, I just got an inheritance and I've got a box back there full of cash, climb back there and grab it and I'll buy lunch. That's how I got the van, too."

The box was full of cash and it didn't have anything under a twenty in it. We ate and drove and after two days, he said, "Do you think you can drive this van?"
I said sure, it's just like driving a big car. So we drove through Kansas and Nebraska and when we got to the other side of Nebraska we were getting pretty bored with this giant cornfield. Just then, on the other side of the freeway, we spotted two girls hitchhiking the other direction. Without much discussion, we got off at the next exit, turned around and headed back up the freeway. When we got up to the girls, we pulled over and asked where they were headed. They said Tennessee, and we said, "So are we!!" We picked them up and headed right back up the freeway the opposite direction we needed to be headed. What guys will do when they meet a pretty girl.

In the end, it took us over two months to finally make it to California. We were headed to Big Bear Lake. Mike's father was a makeup artist at one of the big movie studios, and had a beautiful house up in a very secluded neighborhood. I thought it was strange that no one locked his or her doors. They also all seemed to know each other's names, a very small and tightly knit community. But this wasn't the California I was looking for. So I lasted another two weeks or so and I had to go. I wanted to see Hollywood. I've had slight aspirations to become a poet until I realized you have to die to become famous.

As we traveled across the USA, Mike made it a point to stop at every church that we passed. He was on a serious religion kick, but as long as he didn't push it onto me, more power to him. Religion had never played much of a factor in my life, so at this point of my travels, I didn't have any opinion on religion, unlike now. After all of the different experiences with religion in my life, I think that I understand religion, at least for me, personally.

Many people require a written set of rules, gospels, commandments, etc. to tell them things that they should already know. If writing it down helps them, great. Religion gives people a dream of a better life, in a next life, and I just can't see living my life as if preparing for the next. I live my life like it's my last and when

I leave this earth, I want to be proud of the life that I left behind. When I die, I want to know that I did the right thing in almost every choice I made in life.

People also use religion as a gathering place, like a social event. Hanging out with a large group of people who don't have much more in common with me than the fact that we go to the same church. I never clicked on any other level with any of them. Gathering with the other parishioners after a church service never really left any impression on me at all. I know for a fact that I went to many of them, but I can't actually remember being there or meeting anyone specific. Some things were so dull, I can't remember anything except the fact that it was extremely dull and I couldn't wait to go home.

Religion can be a leaning post when life gets you tired, something to hold onto for support when nothing else seems to be going right. I have never felt that need for support. I believe in myself and that I can accomplish it. I have been able to overcome every adversity, some much slower than others, without needing that support. I pride myself on the fact that I survived this long, leaning on myself when times were tough. That pride may have been the cause of a few of my tribulations, but it is also my pride that carried me through it all to the other side.

Through the years, I've seen many more cons than pros on religion. The negative experiences have caused me to decide that I am better off without it. It would be another obstacle in life to deal with when I have so many others as well.

I traveled from Big Bear Lake to the monstrous metropolis of Los Angeles County by bus. Mike's dad bought me the ticket, probably just to get rid of me. He was angry with Mike for spending so much money and for taking so much time to travel from Michigan, where his adventure began, to Big Bear Lake, where his adventure was to end. He didn't seem to care too much for Mike's new found religion as well. I think he must have assumed that I had something to do with it, which is the furthest from the truth. The bus ticket afforded me a way to travel without having to hitchhike, so I gladly accepted the offer.

The Los Angeles Bus Station has to be one of the seediest, dirtiest places I've ever seen. As well as the normal, day to day life and business of a bus station, it also housed an entire separate community of winos, bag ladies, pimps, drug dealers, homeless people sleeping on benches, and a few of the harmless, mentally deranged that were just above the line of insanity that would require institutionalization. Some of the deranged are teetering right on the edge of that line, only needing a little push in the wrong direction to go tumbling out of reality, into their own little worlds. I would see at least one person like that each day on the streets of Los Angeles and San Francisco. I've even attempted to talk to a few of them, mainly to appease my own curiosity. I wanted to know if they really were as crazy as they appeared, or if it was all just a game.

Let me tell you a little about the different types of people I encountered. They may not all be in Los Angeles, but there are some like them in every town and city.

Some of them, I couldn't communicate with at all. They held full conversations with themselves, usually quite animated and loud. When I tried to start up a conversation, they would stare blankly at me, like I had spoken another language, before going back to their much more interesting conversation with themselves. If I kept trying to talk to them, they'd get frustrated with my interruption and decide that anywhere else is a better than here to continue their private conversation. Streamer Guy was like that.

He was very tall and wore colorful, unusual clothing that was always too small for his long limbs. He had on black horn-rimmed glasses with these long tinsel strands tied to the temples of the glasses. The streamers hung down almost to his belt. His hair was always disheveled, from screaming so much, I bet. He would find a busy intersection, no particular one because over the years, I've seen him in every area of San Francisco. He became a mobile institution, guaranteed to be seen at least once a week somewhere in the city after he found a good spot on the edge of the street, right at the corner, one step away from the curb and sidewalk. Then, for an hour or more, he would stand there and scream obscenities at all of the passing cars. Most of it didn't make sense, just a bunch of cussing. It was like a strange form of Tourrette's Syndrome, one that could be turned on and off like a light switch. Once it was turned on, it was on full power, with just breaks to take a breath.

He became a regular sight in San Francisco, unusual but after seeing it for years on end, it was looked at as another of San Francisco's many hidden forms of entertainment. Years later, each time my wife and I spotted him in the city, we would smile and wave or say hello to Streamer Guy. Most times, he continued his personal rampage, undisturbed by our interruptions. We knew he had heard us, but he was just too busy at the moment.

Three months or so after my daughter's birth my wife and I were out on one of our walks in the city, pushing my daughter's stroller. My wife spotted Streamer Guy on his usual tirade against the evil cars that drove through his city. We waved as we walked by, expecting to be ignored. Instead, he stopped screaming at the cars, walked over to where we were standing, peered down into the stroller and said, "What a beautiful baby."

He turned around and went back out to where he was originally standing and started right where he left off, scolding cars as they drove by... I guess. I really don't know where he left off, since it didn't make any sense. On that day, we knew that our daughter was destined for special and wonderful things in her life. She had been blessed by Streamer Guy. Every time either my daughter's mother or I would be out walking with our baby and come across Streamer Guy, he stopped his rant just to come over and look at the baby. He usually didn't say anything, only stared at her with a little smile on his face. After we passed him by, he would begin his rant again. Strangely, he would wait until we got some distance away from him. Maybe he didn't want to scare the child? It's a nice thought, anyway. You never knew with Streamer Guy.

Diana Ross was another type completely. Diana was more of the drug-induced type. Diana was a small, thin black man who looked no closer to Diana Ross than I did. He had done some sort of serious damage to his vocal cords. His voice was extremely raspy, more like the snow that you hear when you can't find a station on the AM radio. He always carried a high wattage boom-box radio everywhere he went. He would dress up in Diana Ross performance outfits, all sorts of color and glitter. He would find a large, open area, like the civic center. Then, he would crank up his stereo to the top volume, always playing Diana Ross songs, and perform to his invisible audience for hours and hours. Hours of loud Diana Ross singing with this raspy, snowy voice singing every word, loud enough to be heard over the real Diana.

Everyone around the Civic Center knew him and we all called him Diana Ross. He wouldn't respond to anything else and when he introduced himself, it was always as Diana Ross. Everyone in my world knew him because he was a heavy drug user and frequently had large wads of cash. He collected Social Security for being a 'wing-nut' (crazy person), so on the first and fifteenth of each month, he was rich for a quick minute. I began to realize after a few months that Diana's 'performances' were usually on the 1st through 4th and 15th through 19th of each month, right after check day. He only really lost it right after he got paid each time. He would go find a big bag of speed, and proceed to get really, really, really high. After spending hours getting all dressed up for a performance, he would get even higher, right before he left the door of his hotel room. By the time he reached the Civic Center, he'd done enough crank to keep him going for the next three or four days, enough crank to kill any normal person.

So, I discovered that his insanity was drug induced, but it was enough for the government to certify him as crazy. He probably went to all of his psychiatrist meetings high as a kite. I've talked to him on days that it was obvious that he wasn't high and he seemed normal and grouchy. He may have been a bit odd, but not enough to label insane, until performance nights.

The tragic end to Diana was the fact that too many people knew when Diana received money. The wrong person or people found out, which was eventually going to happen. They found Diana dead in his hotel room from a 'hot-shot'. A 'hot-shot' is a scary word in this world. I was one of the very few dope fiends that didn't use a needle. Almost every other person I knew used one. When someone doesn't like you, they are just evil, or like in Diana's case, they want to rip you off, they mix up a hit in a syringe. The hit contains something other than dope. I've heard stories of people using Drano and other types of powdered poison. Whatever is in that syringe, it's poison and it kills the person who uses it. I've heard of it happening a few times, usually to someone who fucked over some spun out 'crankster-gangster', as they liked to be called. 'Crankster gangsters' had ties to all the big drug dealers and didn't take lightly to getting fucked over and stolen from. But, Diana didn't fuck anyone over; he just had a large roll of money in front of the wrong person. He never deserved that, he only wanted to get high and sing.

The Los Angeles bus station was the last place in the world that I wanted to be. I was seventeen years old and brand new to this crazy California lifestyle. I got out of there quickly, trying not to stare, but not really succeeding. How can I not be curious when I see a guy in a bright colored suit and lots of jewelry walk up and start talking to some girl with a backpack who looks sixteen years old and fresh off the bus from Iowa. What could he possibly be up to but no good?

The Los Angeles County Bus Transit system was massive and all encompassing. It crisscrossed every main street in L.A. and some bus routes were four hours long from beginning to end. I found the ones that ran the circuit late at night and got on at the beginning of the route. I would go all the way to the back of the bus and sleep until the end of the route, when the driver usually changed and they woke me up. After four hours of solid sleep and the crisp 4 A.M. L.A. air to wake me up, I didn't need any more sleep.

Wandering the streets of L.A. was lonely but never boring. Every time I turned around, something new and interesting was happening. I tried to not get involved, while I watched things unfold from a safe distance away. It was like watching a movie and the actors were really good. There was a lot of arguing in L.A., so everywhere I looked, there was something interesting going on. Being homeless on the street wasn't as tough as it sounds, but after a few weeks of cruising the bus lines and sleeping in 'squats' (abandoned buildings), it started to get old.

I found a church. Michael taught me this one. It was a brand new, massive building that took up over half a city block. I went inside, up to the reception desk, and told the lady sitting there that I was new to the city and homeless. I wanted to know if they could help.

At the time, I didn't look at it as taking advantage of their generosity. I was homeless and wanted to rectify that problem. Now that I look back on it, I must have taken some kind of advantage of them because I can't even remember what religion they were.

They were very kind and giving people. Within an hour after walking in the door, they gave me a bag full of groceries. One of them took me home and let me sleep in a guest room for four days. Four days was as long as I lasted. When I wasn't at the house, where religious TV, bible reading and bible discussions were the norm, I sat at the church, where they sang songs, read the bible and sat around talking about God. In the four days that I lasted, I didn't meet one person who had any goals, dreams, or aspirations. They were serving God, twenty-four/seven, and nothing else, unless they said that they intended to be musicians. They would be musicians for God and their earnings would come back to the church. It seemed kind of cultish to me, like everything in life was centered around the church. It didn't take long for me to realize that this wasn't the place for me. I had a full stomach, a set of semi-new clothes (new to me), and when I told one guy that I was planning to leave, he even gave me a few bucks to get me by.

I wandered around the downtown area of Los Angeles for another week, when someone I was talking to asked if I had seen the ocean. I had never seen the ocean, and I was way too close to not go see it now. So just like that, I found a bus that said Venice beach and jumped on it. By this time, I realized that a bus pass was the way to go, since I traveled by bus every day. Buying a pass once a month was much more convenient and cheaper in the end.

When the bus finally arrived at the last stop on its route, the first thing I noticed was the smell. The salt air was like nothing I had ever smelled before. Of course, it smelled salty, but it also smelled fresh, clean, and sort of damp or misty. Sometimes, walking along the beach, you can get wet from the mist. The bus stop was three blocks from the ocean, but I could easily see the ocean from there. I purposely didn't look at the ocean until I got all the way down to the beach. Once I got past all the expensive bungalow houses right along the beachfront, I stopped and just stared. For what seemed like forever, but must have been at least fifteen minutes, I just stood and stared.

I stood in front of the most massive thing in the world. I could feel the raw power vibrate in the sand from the surge of each wave, watching how each wave affected the sand, all the way down the beach, as far as the eye could see in either direction. There was more water in front of me than land behind me that I stood upon. I've hitchhiked across more than three quarters of this landmass, so I could appreciate exactly how big it was. Not to mention, how deep it wass, with a whole different type of world going on deep inside it. It was just massive; there is no other way to describe it.

I took off my socks and shoes, rolled up my pants legs and walked down through the wet sand. It was a sensation like no other, feeling wet sand squishing up between my toes, gooey wet and sandy solid at the same time. As I stepped into the cold ocean water, I couldn't help myself; I needed to go further in. In no time, I was up to my waist in the water, feeling the currents pulling my legs and feet in one direction, while the waves rolling in pushed the rest of me the opposite direction. I could feel the sheer power of the ocean and I wasn't even very far away from shore. While I was busy studying the power of the ocean, a larger than normal wave came in and covered me from head to toe. A feeling of not knowing which way was up enveloped me, but it was just for a split second before the wave was past me and headed for shore. All that I could do was stand there, soaking wet, and laugh. It's not that I had anything better to do than walk around Venice Beach and dry off. Plus, for an added bonus, I got my first taste of ocean salt water. It wasn't as bad as I expected, but it was obvious that I couldn't survive on it if I had to. Just that little swallow made me thirsty.

So I tramped around Hollywood, learning how to survive on the streets. It wasn't like there weren't hundreds of homeless people around here. You can't truly go hungry unless you refuse to go eat at one of the free meal establishments, mostly at shelters and churches. There was a Denny's around there that I spent many a night at, almost all night drinking coffee and eating something really cheap. There was a very pretty waitress who worked there and she never hassled me if I was there. If I fell asleep she would wake me up right at the end of her shift, before the new crew came on. She reminded me of the one girl back in St. Charles that I truly missed. They looked a lot alike but there was more to it than that

One of the main reasons for writing this story is as a forum. Maybe I was just seeing my old sweetheart in her because it made me miss her a little less. Maybe it's partially an apology for what I've done, and to at least make her understand that all the writing I did to her in the past was completely from the heart, and if she reads this, she'll see how honest I've been. Although I didn't tell her everything, I didn't tell anyone everything. It would have been way too long and involved. I'll just have to write it in a book.

One night I was sitting in Denny's and it had to be at least midnight. I was doing the coffee all nighter and I had my notepad with me. I had started writing things down again. It helped to reflect back and to remember where my head was at during a certain situation. Two tables over there was this little elf of a guy who had an Albert Einstein hairdo. He seemed all enwrapped in something that at least he felt was very important. The guy sitting with him didn't seem to share his intensity. So when my favorite waitress came back to refill my coffee cup for the umpteenth time, I asked her if she knew who he was or what his story was. She said that she didn't know his name but that she was sure that he was a Hollywood writer. She also said that he came in there a lot and we had both been in here at the same time many times before. I just never noticed him because I was so wrapped up in my notebook. Now I wanted to know about him. I wanted to know what the writing business was like. So I went over and introduced myself, my lack of fear paying off again.

I said, "Hi! I've been told that you're a big time writer in Hollywood."

The guy sitting next to him kind of snickered. I could tell I took him by surprise, but I wasn't gonna let up, "I've dreamed of being a writer in Hollywood and I want to know how you started out."

He said very pleasantly, "No I don't consider myself a big time writer, but I do dabble a bit, and yes, I've seen you here before and you always seem to be writing. So what exactly are you asking me to let you in on? Some secret to making it big? I wish I knew that one myself."

At about this time, his much younger friend said he had to go and asked if I'd like to take his seat. As soon as he was out of earshot, the writer leaned over and said, "He's an up and coming actor but he's really just an asshole. Unfortunately, those are the ones that usually make it. This is definitely a nice guy finishes last business."

We sat and talked for over an hour and I asked him if he had written anything I might have seen. He had but there weren't that many that I had heard of. I had heard of a few. I asked him what he was working on then, and he told me he was rewriting a story about a girl who gets mixed up in drugs and the bad life and eventually kills herself. He was turning it into a movie script.

Then he shot back, "What may I ask are you presently working on?"

I told him that I was trying to write a few new poems, that I hadn't written one in a few years. He asked if I had any of my poetry with me. I told him that I had a poem I wrote in high school that I thought was my best work so far. He asked to read it, so he read 'A Letter to God'. It's a poem about suicide and I can still remember it to this day, but it's not for this story. I don't think I would have even let him read it if I didn't think it might help me get his attention and possibly his help. He was quiet for a few seconds and then asked, "Do you mind if I get a copy of this? I might be able to get this put in the movie."

I was ecstatic that he liked it, let alone wanted to do something with it. So I said, "Sure, I'll just give you this copy, I've got it memorized anyway."

Within three months of seeing him twice or so a week, he came in with the final draft of the script. It was a very good story, and it was going to do well. He told me that at the end of the movie before they run the credits, they were going to scroll my poem up the screen. I was very excited to see it up there and when I finally did, it just floored me how big it looked. He took me to a special screening of it with a bunch of people I didn't know, but he knew all of them. The movie was way before it's time and it would have done a lot better ten years later, people didn't like to see the main character die in the end. About two weeks after that he just stopped coming to Denny's. I still dropped by every couple of nights to see if he was there, but he never came back.

One night I came in after being gone more than a week and my favorite waitress was there. When I sat down she came over and sat down across from me. She usually only did that after three in the morning when no one else was around. She looked really sad so I asked her what was wrong. She said that young actor guy, who I met with our writer friend, came in to the diner and told her that he died two months ago of a heart attack, that he was surprised we hadn't heard and that it was on TV. Neither of us owned a TV so I could understand how we missed that news story. She said he really looked sorry though and felt so bad about being the one to break the news that he left almost immediately. My favorite waitress wanted to know how I was taking it, but I couldn't really respond because I wasn't sure how I was taking it. I just knew that no matter how sad it was, I doubted that I would shed one tear. That just made me angry. The anger was finally beginning to bubble over. Finally I had a chance and with another cruel twist of fate, it all came to an end. So I told her that I was going out for a walk and I never went back there. It was just all too much.

I went to a payphone and called home collect. I hadn't attempted to contact my family since I had left and it had been a long while. I talked to my sister and told her that I was in Hollywood. She was very nice and caring, which wasn't how I remembered her from before. That kind of spooked me; then she started telling me about the things going on around my family back there. It seemed that they had enough to worry about, and maybe this wasn't such a good idea to call, at least not a good time. So I got out of the phone booth and didn't call back for a long while. I'm sorry that I don't have time lines down very well, but it was a lot of stuff crammed into a small amount of time. I should ask my sister; I bet she'll remember.

CHAPTER 3
LIFE SPEEDS UP

I found my way up to North Hollywood where I met a guy in a park and we became really good friends. I didn't know about his drug habit at the beginning, but I doubt it really would have mattered. I think that was the least of my concerns. I had a place to stay; now I just had to find a job. I looked all over the place, and went to the Employment Development Department. I remember that it was just before Thanksgiving, and the Employment Development Department sent me to the Honeybake ham store.

I got there and was handed a torch and a box of sticks of sugar and told I had to glaze these hams. I had no idea what I was doing but I gave it a try. The sugar crackled and exploded a lot because it was burning, and I got hit by flying sugar about fifteen to twenty times when I said screw this, this isn't even worth staying for my check. I just took off my short gloves and walked out. Now back to trying to find a real job. I tried being a busboy at a restaurant but that wasn't my gig either. I dropped a few dishes and I'm sure eventually I would have gotten the hang of it, but I would have hated it. A waiter made more money, but then I would have to pretend to be nice to people who are being rude to me. Nope, can't see that ever happening again.

Jobs came and went but nothing interested me for very long. Then one day my roommate got me high on meth and I don't think I truly came down from it for six years, give or take a year. I told you before that my time line can get pretty screwy. I just know it all fit into the years of 1985 to 2001. I'm just not sure how. I stayed up for three days the first time that I got high and I couldn't shut the hell up. Sometimes I just talked to myself. It was really a bad experience, but at the same time, it was easy to see how addicting it could become. Over the course of the next six years, almost every meth user I knew shot up with a needle. I was a unique breed because I just snorted it. It's probably the only reason I've outlived every one of them and actually got off it. I may have been addicted to the drug, but there was also an addiction to that needle that I never had to endure. Once someone uses a needle, he will go to all extremes to avoid doing the drug any other way. I've seen them try and try again, making a human pin cushion out of themselves, and just hoping someone will show up that can hit them, because I sure as hell can't.

After managing to get good and strung out for a few months, I decided I needed to get away from the speed crowd and find new friends. I had one gay friend in Hollywood, Tony, which was new for me because I had never met an openly gay person before.
I was very impressed about his openness and honesty, and I was very up front

that I had just never found a guy attractive, and how a beautiful woman gives me a feeling that no guy has ever given me. He never once made any advances, which is good because I don't know how I would have reacted. It would have pissed me off that he used our friendship to try for something more, but he never gave me that impression. Plenty of others during those six years have made offers and suggestions, but that's the price you pay in the speed crowd. A large part of it was gay, so you had to be at least friendly, but I didn't put up with any shit either.

Tony had seen that I was coming apart at the seams. He told me one day that he was going to go back to his lover in Santa Rosa and I was welcome to come along, no strings attached, just a place to stay away from Hollywood. I asked what his lover was like and he said he was an older man old enough to be his father but he has a large house and I'd have a room and no one would bother me. Santa Rosa is way up in the northern part of California, far away from these tweakers and this meth. Yeah right, Santa Rosa is also a college town full of young women who are all about drinking and partying.

It took me about a month in Santa Rosa to find a couple girls that needed a roommate, and no matter how much Tony said I wasn't imposing, I still felt like I needed to move out. Tony and his lover were fighting and I just didn't want to hear one day that I started some kind of fight between them, just by living there. So meeting the girls was good timing. Cheryl had two little monsters for children, but they changed after a while, when someone showed them a little attention. Stephanie did beer commercials and was drop dead gorgeous. It was a fun living arrangement and I watched Cheryl's kids as well as got a job at the mall on the other side of the freeway. At first I got a job at a fast food chain, but when I heard they were hiring in the maintenance department, I asked to go on my break and ran down there to talk them into hiring me. It didn't take much talking, they saw I was interested and they needed someone right away.

I went home that night and told Cheryl and Stephanie, and to celebrate Stephanie pulled out a bag of speed. Oh boy, here we go again. Stephanie seemed to have an endless supply of it from when she made the commercials. So all those days started blurring again in a constant state of spun-out confusion.

Sonny was Cheryl's on again off again boyfriend. He showed up for a few days at a time and then he was gone again for weeks on end. He claimed to be affiliated with a large motorcycle club, but I never really saw any type of proof. I only met three of his friends but none of them seemed the Harley riding type. He would pop into town, stay at our place, do one or two big drug deals, and then off again to another destination in California.

Sonny had been staying with us for a couple of days when he asked me if I wanted to go on a road trip to get some pot. It would take two days and I was up for something new and exciting. I wasn't exactly sure what a road trip with Sonny would entail, but I was high enough to partake in the adventure. It didn't take any convincing at all; I wanted to get out of the house and see more of California.

We packed up his little, two-seater sports car and headed up north along the Pacific Coast Highway, heading for Fort Bragg. Pacific Coast Highway is a twisting highway that runs the entire coast of California. The Pacific Ocean is on one side of you and a rocky cliff side on the other. At some points, it runs right next to the water. You can find beautiful views all along your drive. There are many vista points to stop, take pictures and stretch your legs. We didn't even slow down for any of the stops, and I didn't have much of a chance to enjoy the views.

Sonny drove like a maniac. We raced at between eighty and a hundred miles an hour the entire way, sometimes, more than a hundred, if the opportunity presented itself. I just held on for dear life with my eyes closed most of the ride. It was like riding a roller coaster when you knew there were no safety precautions. What I did see during our drive went by in such a blur; I still didn't see very much.

We drove over a long bridge, high above a town that I assumed was Fort Bragg. Sonny pointed to a mobile home trailer park, down below the bridge, right along the ocean. That was our final destination. I was just glad that Sonny finally slowed down to the posted speed limit.

The trailer park was full of Harley motorcycles and pit bulls. Everywhere I looked, laundry hung out in front of homes with a dog or two sleeping underneath it. Like someone would steal their laundry and they felt the need to protect it? We stopped at a specific trailer, parked the car, and went inside.

It looked like any other white trash household, empty beer cans scattered around and dirty dishes in the sink. Sonny talked to a big, burly guy for about fifteen minutes before he handed Sonny three trash bags loaded down with pot. He had to hand them one bag at a time since he only had one arm. I'll be the first to admit that I was too scared to ask him how he lost his arm, but I bet it was a great story. Tomorrow was my birthday and I wanted to live to see it. Like many pivotal points in my life, I stayed smart and kept my mouth shut.
When Sonny said that he was going to pick up some pot, I didn't expect it to fill the entire storage compartment of the car we were driving. He even had to take the spare tire out for more room. Hopefully, we wouldn't be needing that!

Now, we were off to Turlock to drop the load off. The only thing I could think about the whole ride was how much trouble we would be in if we got pulled over because Sonny was driving like a lunatic. The entire car reeked of pot. The police officer would probably get stoned when he leaned in to get Sonny's driver's license.

Turlock was a very small town south of Fort Bragg and far inland, so at least I didn't have to hold onto the seat as we squealed around curves along a cliff side, high above the ocean. It was far enough away that we stopped for the night at a cheap motel and slept.

The next morning was my birthday and Sonny said that he had a surprise for me. He took me to a Mexican friend of his in town that did tattoos. I got my first real tattoo in Turlock. I already had a couple of ink stains on my arm from when I was a kid, trying to tattoo myself with my best friend Eric. I used a needle wrapped with a piece of string back then and some ink my mom used for calligraphy. My birthday tattoo says 'comfortably numb' and has two roses intertwined with barbed wire. It is on my upper right arm and I still like it, even to this day.

After the tattoo and the drop off of pot at another of Sonny's friends, we headed back to Santa Rosa and I had a permanent memory that will be impossible to ever forget. I can look at the tattoo and remember those times. Whether the memories are good, bad, or mixed, they were memories from my past experience that shaped who I became. Sonny hung around for a couple more days in Santa Rosa but he had important business elsewhere and had to leave town in a rush. There was never any warning with Sonny.

I met a large number of college girls and they were all willing to try a little meth, so life was great for a while. I thought nothing could go wrong there, I was having too much fun. I was meeting girls, which was totally different than back in Missouri. I told you there was only really one back there, but she meant more to me than any of these.

The problem that I was creating was that I was spinning a web of lies in order to date more than one girl at once. I guess I thought I had a lot of making up to do. But I didn't stop to consider the ramifications. What if they found out? I guess I'd just have a few girls pissed at me.
After so long without a girl, this all came on pretty fast. I just didn't know when to put it to a stop. So fate did it for me, or maybe it was karma.

I met Serena, who wasn't like all the wild college girls. She was sweet and innocent and had just moved to California from Idaho. She never mentioned what her father did for a living, but they lived in a huge house in an upper class neighborhood. We started talking at the mall and I finally talked her into going out on a date with me. It was one of those long processes that when it came through, you felt like you had truly accomplished something. So taking her out on a date was very important to me. After the first date I knew that she wasn't like any other girl I knew and I probably will never meet someone as sweet and down to earth as this girl. We dated for two weeks and I didn't even try to kiss her. I didn't want to screw everything up so I just kept my distance, thinking that otherwise I might scare her away.

After two weeks, I took her back to my house after seeing a movie. She had been over there before, but this time no one else happened to be home. When we got in the house and sat down, she kissed me. I was truly caught off guard, but I managed to recover enough to kiss her back. It was a slow, wonderful night where I did nothing to advance the tempo. I just let her run the show. After the evening was over, she told me that it was her first time, and that she didn't want it to be the last. I felt so touched all I could do was hug and kiss her. She left and said she would come by after work. I told her I'd meet her here, but that she might beat me here. She said that was fine and she'd just wait.

I got off work and headed home, totally unaware what I was about to walk in on. When I got to my house, there were four girls sitting outside my door and I had slept with all of them in the past two months. I knew I was in trouble but I didn't really care about what any of them were feeling except Serena. I hadn't seen any of these girls since Serena and I had started dating but it was a pretty close window there. And it was obvious that it didn't matter. I stood there while I got chewed out by three women all at the same time. I couldn't do anything except accept that I fucked up and this was the result. I wanted to tell them I was sorry, but I really wasn't. They were all wild and crazy party girls who I'm sure were dating other guys as well. They were just pissed because they felt I wasn't up front with them.

Serena didn't say a word; she just waited for the rest to have there say and for them to leave. Then she just stood there staring at me. I stood quiet for a minute then tried to tell her that they were totally different than her, and that I wasn't what she envisioned me to be. She just stood there for a few more seconds, took a step forward, and slapped me. Then she said, "If I were you I'd watch out for my daddy." She turned around and walked away.
Two weekends later Cheryl and Stephanie were having a party at the house, and I just happened to come home from a friend's house right when the beer ran out. I said I'd go along on the beer run. While we were gone Serena's daddy showed up at the house on his Harley Davidson with a few friends who were all wearing

the same Hell's Angels leather vests. He went through the party with a gun and pistol-whipped three people looking for me. He was sure I was there because someone from the party that had left told him I was. He rampaged around for a while longer and then he left with his buddies in tow. When I got back with the beer, no one was in the partying mood anymore. Needless to say I packed up my backpack again and decided it was in my best interest to leave town as soon as possible. I left the house that night, feeling a little twinge of something I hadn't felt in a while, fear. It was time to move on, I saw no nice ending here.

So I went to the Salvation Army for a cot to sleep on and a meal in the morning before I moved out to the freeway to start hitching a ride out of town. That was where I met Gary, my new soon to be road dog. I had a few very close friends that vanished without a trace throughout my life and Gary was one of them.

CHAPTER 4
POT - WIELDING FIENDS

The next morning we packed up our bags and headed to the freeway right after we ate breakfast. Gary told me that he and his wife split up and that he was going to see a friend in San Francisco. He asked if I'd ever been there; I told him not anywhere except Fisherman's Wharf once. He told me I'd be surprised to find that there's a whole different life in San Francisco, one that most people don't see. He made it sound kind of mysterious and inviting. It was strangely prophetic instead. We talked and walked all day long and no one even slowed down, let alone stopped. When it started getting dark and cars didn't even see us until it was too late for them to stop, we decided to head back into the woods and sleep under some trees. We walked pretty far back into the woods until we couldn't hear the cars anymore, and settled down in the dark. We talked a bit more before we fell asleep. Gary said he was going to San Francisco because his friend there was fired from the mint, and when he left, he supposedly took a whole bunch of money paper with the fibers in it, and the ingredients to the ink. Sounded a little far fetched to me, but he still sounded so serious about it. Everything changed the next morning anyway.

I don't know which one of us woke up first, but I think we woke up at almost the same time. We sat up stretching, looked around, and realized we had spent the night in a pot field, a pretty big pot field. We looked at each other and then dumped out both our packs, leaving all our clothes in a big pile by the tree we slept under. We stuffed both packs full and barely made a dent in the amount that was there. We ran back to the freeway and caught a ride on a truck right after we got out of the woods. One second we were there, the next we were gone. The truck reeked of diesel fuel, so you couldn't smell the pot, even in the amount we had.

We were dropped off at the Golden Gate Bridge and walked across the bridge into the city. I would never have guessed I'd fall in love with this city, the bad areas and the good, depending on my frame of mind at the time. For being a city six miles wide and seven miles tall, it sure has its allure. It's nice to have everything so close together, yet having neighborhoods that are so different from each other. You can walk a few blocks and you'll be in a whole different world. The city also completely changes from day to night. An area can be full of people during the day, but when the sun sets and the freaks begin to climb out from under their rocks, that same area can turn into a ghost town.

Here's one thing I'll never understand. There was a completely different world inside San Francisco during the night. A seedy world full of freaks and dope-fiends, and it was huge.

I met hundreds of people who you wouldn't want to take home to your mother. Some of them might not be committing criminal acts, but they all had criminal minds. They all thought the same way and it wasn't a very nice way. The police knew about this world, as well as the city government and its friends, but they never did much about it. The entire network of addicts and criminals mainly stayed in a five-block by five-block area called the Tenderloin. That was a joke, that area was more like the week old ground beef. At any time the powers that be could have just swept down each block and taken us all away. But they never did. They knew we were there, so they arrested a token person now and then, but they could have cleaned that whole area out in one day if they really wanted to.

We walked down Lombard Street and saw lots of tourists, motels, and restaurants. It made me uncomfortable to be around so many people with our backpacks full of pot, so we walked down a few streets to Green Street. We zigzagged through the city streets until we made it down to Civic Center Plaza at Seventh Street and Market. We walked onto the brick plaza by about five or six in the evening. I wasn't sure what the plan was but Gary seemed to have some kind of plan, no matter how half-assed.

The Civic Center had a fountain, a grassy area, and a huge concrete plaza area with benches. There was a flurry of people rushing past me, like they had places to be and people to see. But there was also an undercurrent of people just milling around, hanging out, or maybe waiting for someone. Almost all of the benches had people sitting on them, talking to friends, feeding pigeons, or reading. On one of the benches sat a haggardly looking old man with a fishing cap on. He had a forty-ounce bottle of beer wrapped in a paper bag and looked like he'd fight anyone who tried to take it from him. Gary nudged me in the ribs and nodded over to the old guy with the beer. He started walking over there, so I just followed. I did a lot of following in the beginning, but the real money was in the leading.

We sat down on both sides of the guy and Gary introduced us to him. I saw his hand tighten on his bottle as soon as we got close to him. He said his name was John and asked what we wanted. "Are you lookin'?"

Gary asked, "Looking for what? What can you get us? Can you get us some KGB?"

John looked totally puzzled, "KGB?"

Gary smiled; he had him now, "Yeah, KGB, that stands for killer green bud. You know where to find any for cheap?"

John frowned, "Nah, all you can get around here is brown Mexican that they call Thai stick. But it is really cheap and it does the trick in a pinch."

Gary asked coyly, "Hey John, wanna smoke a joint?"

We smoked a little of the pot with John and he was very impressed. He asked if we could get more, that he knew people who would want some. Now Gary pounced, "You don't say? Yeah I think our connection might have more of this."

Well, that was my first lesson in drug dealing. Never let a dope fiend know that you are the man. Let them think you have to get it from someone else. It gives you more flexibility, because fiends want their dope NOW. It also makes it harder for the fiend to come up with a plan to rob you or rip you off.

Now Gary was on a roll, "You know, John, you said you could turn over some of this? I might be able to set up a deal with you. How 'bout you sell four dimes for me, I'll give you one? I'll front you five bags of KGB and you give me forty dollars. Plus every time we see each other, I'll get you fucked up."

I saw dollar signs in John's eyes, and the promise of constant free highs was a great incentive. The bonus theory in business works well in this line of work. But John was still a little confused, "But I don't have forty dollars."

Gary told him, "I said I'd front it to you, I'll come back later to pick up my forty dollars."

John was all for this deal. Gary told John that he didn't have any baggies for the pot but next time, it would be all bagged up for him. We gave John enough pot to make five dimes out of, and were getting ready to leave when two guys walked up and asked if anyone knew where they could find some pot. Gary immediately spoke up, "Nope, sorry buddy, I can't help you out there."

After the guys walked off, he looked over to John and nodded after them. John got up and chased after them while we sat at the bench and watched what was going on across the plaza. Gary said, "You let them take the chance, we got the supply."

I had a few questions to this logic, though. I thought I'd wait until we left there. I had a feeling we were getting ready to go. John walked back over to us and the two guys walked the other direction with their pleasant surprise of green bud. John sat at the bench with us and slipped some money to Gary. He did it with one smooth motion and if you weren't looking for it, you never would have seen it.

All the sudden I saw how this business was going to be. At first I thought it was just a form of paranoia, but after awhile I realized that some people really were watching. Not all of them, actually very few of them, were cops. Everyone in this lifestyle wants to know everything. Knowledge is power, and there is a large gossip grapevine. Tweakers love to talk, not always telling the truth, but just to hear their own voices. They make things up thinking that if they give you a little tidbit of gossip, it'll put them in your good graces. That's just a theory, but it does come from what I've witnessed. They say that the three fastest forms of communication are telephone, telegraph, and tell-a-tweaker. That is very true; if you don't want something known by everyone, then don't tell anyone.

John said to us, "There's twenty bucks so I owe you twenty more, right?"

Gary nodded, "Yep, twenty and we'll be even. I'll be back in a couple hours, will you be here?"

John said, "Yeah, I'll be here and I'll have your other twenty by then, so bring me five more, OK?"

"Sure thing, I'll be back with that and I'll roll up a fatty to smoke you out, like I promised. See you then John."

Gary was up and headed out of the plaza before I even noticed. I bounced up off the bench and caught up with him half a block down. He told me, "You gotta get in and get out as quickly as possible. The longer you are in one place, the better the odds were that you'll be noticed by someone else."

Gary studied the odds of everything. It's a habit I picked up from him, and sometimes I wish I hadn't. Playing everything according to the odds means taking no chances in life. Sometimes you gotta take chances if you want something.

Two blocks away from the Civic Center, he pulled two ten dollar bills out of his pocket and said, "Now we gotta buy baggies and get a hotel room so we can bag up some of this bud. This should be just about enough. These slum hotels are only about fifteen a night, and as soon as possible, we'll rent a room for a week. It's a lot cheaper that way."

While we walked to the head shop that sold drug paraphernalia, I figured I'd ask my questions, "OK, I've got a couple questions here. First off, what's gonna keep that guy in the fisherman's hat from just walking off with that dope and just never seeing us again? Seems kinda stupid to just give our pot away like that. Second question is about the comment of letting them take the chance. You are still taking a chance just by being associated with them, but if you did it yourself, you'd make a lot more money." Gary looked at me and realized that this had gone from winging it to an actual business partnership. He said, "His name is John, the guy in the hat."

"OK, Fisherman John," I nicknamed him.

Gary finished, "Well, if you are going to front someone drugs, never front more than you can afford to lose. You saw how much we gave him; it wasn't even a spit in the barrel. So I don't really care if he's there or not, but if he is, I'll be twenty dollars richer. Sometimes you are going to lose, either they are gonna run off or get busted, but if they think that you'll front them more when they get out of jail, they won't be inclined to tell on you. But the odds tell me that this is the safest way for me to operate. Selling it yourself is more dangerous. Not only the danger of getting arrested, but the danger of getting robbed or killed over some dope. So you will make more money, but it balances out with the chances you take."

"So to be safe and make money, you have to deal in large volume?" I asked.

"Yeah but that has its problems too. You can't always get large amounts, you have to transport large amounts, and you have to hide large amounts. That can prove to be a pain in the ass," he explained.

We went to a seedy looking hotel in the Tenderloin, only three blocks down from the plaza. The room had cockroaches and a sink in it and no bathroom. The sheets were dirty and the blanket had a big hole in it. Paint was cracked and peeling on all the walls and some spots had little tags of graffiti from previous tenants. The window was painted black and you couldn't see out of it. I later discovered that there was a flashing neon sign right outside, and this must have been their solution to the complaints from tenants of the light flashing all night long. This was as low as you could probably get for a room. Gary said that as soon as we made a little more money, we'd get a room with a bathroom. So I asked, "Where am I supposed to piss?" I learned that when you rent a room without a bathroom, everyone on the entire floor shares one or two bathrooms and a bathtub. Wonderful! I didn't even know what kind of freaks I would be sharing these things with. Wino's, dope fiends, hookers, and the mentally disturbed are the usual fare in one of these hotels. Sometimes all wrapped up into one very strange person.

So for a few weeks things ran smoothly. But he was still obsessed with this plan of his to learn how to print money, and to get this money paper from his friend. He talked me into taking a print shop course with him at San Francisco City College. I think I took it only because I've always liked learning, and Gary wouldn't have been as driven to actually go if I wasn't there with him. But I had yet to meet this money-paper person or see this ink recipe.

A couple weeks later he brought home a single piece of paper that had red and blue threads all throughout it, so I started to see that he might actually follow through on this plot.

Gary said he knew someone in the Haight-Ashbury area who he could buy bud from, when our enormous supply ran out. That came very quickly. I asked what the Haight-Ashbury area was and was told that it was the hippie area of San Francisco. There's a great big park at the end of Haight Street and it was full of people who either never let the sixties move on, or people too young to remember the sixties who wanted to try to live that lifestyle. When young people aren't happy with their lifestyle or when they have it forced on them by their parents, they are willing to try just about any other lifestyle as long as it's different. And the 'happy hippy' lifestyle is pretty inviting. Partying all the time, no rent, lots of 'family', and everybody shares everything (except maybe their stash).

One night, two weeks before our graduation from printing school, Gary said he was going to the Haight to see his friend and wanted to know if I had any money so he could get there. He'd given all his money to his friend earlier that day and was waiting to go pick up the bud. I told him no, I didn't have any money, but I had one bus token. It would get him there but he'd need to find another way back. He said no problem. He'd be back in an hour or two. He never came back.

CHAPTER 5
SAY NO TO POT

My hotel was paid for a little over two more weeks. But I was broke and I didn't have very much pot. Well, I couldn't solve this problem inside a hotel room. I went to the only place I knew I could make some quick cash, the Civic Center. I walked down there thinking about how I was going to get started, because I knew that I had to do something.

As soon as I got down there, I recognized a few people from the past month or two. Fisherman John was down there and as soon as he saw me, he made a beeline right to me. So much for not being noticed. He wanted to know, "Where's Gary, because there are some people who want pot and Gary was supposed to be down here last night.

I told him, "Gary never came back last night and I don't know what happened to him. I have a few bags but I need all the cash I can get for it because it's all I've got left."

John looked completely devastated, his gravy train was gone, but he said, "Well there's a girl over there and a guy over there who want some bud, go get their money. When things are looking up for you again, remember that I never ripped you off." So I went and got their money and then I had to figure out what to do next.

That's when I met this big American Indian named Stan. He looked American Indian, but he talked and acted like a spoiled upper middle class white kid. He talked a lot about when he played football. We talked and drank a beer and I told him what happened to me and my vanishing friend. He said he didn't have anywhere to live either and needed to get something going. We talked about selling pot to survive and even tried it for a while, but we both smoked way too much to make any profit from it. So we needed something new. We started selling meth and the money started doubling. Every single time we went to get more, our financial situation had increased. We figured we could make a shitload of money selling meth while only smoking pot. Needless to say, that didn't happen for long. Soon it became like that commercial, I did more speed, to stay up longer, to make more money, to do more speed..... But we had cash now.

When I look back at it now, I can see the allure at the beginning and how it sucked me into it so quickly. I had lots of money, a big bag of drugs, and all sorts of women. What more can a guy ask for, especially at nineteen? I was still mentally a post high school student. I'm not making excuses, I'm just explaining

where my head was at that moment.
It doesn't mean that it was in a good place. At this point things may jump around a bit but they are all coming back to the same place. I'm climbing up the ladder of drug dealing, and it's a ride that you wouldn't believe.

I moved out of the slum hotel, mainly because the rent Gary and I paid on it ran out. I just couldn't see myself paying more money for a place like that. I didn't sleep much, so I didn't really need a room. It was just another expense for a place that I was hardly ever at.

Stan and I began our insane quest through San Francisco. We stayed high all the time, either on meth or the new drug we found in the Haight, LSD. Acid warped our views on everything around us, but it also had that speedy effect like meth. If it weren't for the fear that our minds might permanently be damaged by the constant use of acid, it probably would have become our drug of choice. We experimented with all sorts of different types of drugs and drug combinations. We discovered that large quantities of orange juice intensified the acid trips. So we would buy gallons of the stuff at the local farmer's market. One night we drank so much orange juice, that when the LSD finally started to kick in, the strychnine in the acid caused us to throw-up. That was a truly bad trip. Vomiting in techno-color was not as cool as it might sound. And it was definitely an experience a person wouldn't soon forget.

We stayed around the Civic Center area because that's where the money was, unless we went up to the Haight, but there were way too many cops up there. The police department left us alone in the downtown area but they were on a major crackdown of the Haight Ashbury area. On every corner were uniformed police officers, as well as undercover officers all over the place. They really had it out for the dirty ole hippy. As long as we didn't have dread locks or wore patched together clothing, the police didn't give us a second glance up there. But I bet the moment we would have tried to wheel and deal our wares, they would have been on us like a pack of wolves. So we kept it down at the Civic Center, where it was moderately safe.

There was one little hippy we loved to run into. His name was hippy Roy and he was always a sight to see. If it wasn't his loudly clashing, color filled clothing, or the fact that he was always barefoot that you first noticed about him, it was the rainbow beanie with the propeller on top that gave him away. He was obviously "the man" when it came to LSD. He had these doses called "golden acorns" because of the gold leaf acorn print on each individual hit of acid. He would only sell Stan and me three each at a time because he said any more would hurt us. I figured that if being hurt was ending up like Roy, I didn't want to get that hurt. He was a nice enough guy, but there was definitely something whacked about him.

He always appeared out of nowhere, although he did all of his traveling on foot. After he sold us a few doses, he disappeared the exact same way, like a phantom. Since he was barefoot, he didn't make any noise when he walked. Down in the plaza, you could always hear when someone was coming, from the echo across the empty area of his shoes or boots. That was a major benefit for both Stan and me because we were both blind as a bat. That was one of our running jokes, about how we'd never be able to run from the police because neither of us would see them until they were right up on us. But it didn't stop us from seeing all the drama unfolding around us.

I remember one night, there was a skinny little tweaker named Bruce sitting up on a concrete wall, where way below the entrance to BART (Bay Area Rapid Transit) opened up. Stan had just finished telling me some gossip about how this really big guy we both knew was looking for Bruce because he was screwing around with the big guy's girlfriend (just more gossip about the freaks in the neighborhood.) Then Stan pointed over to this shadow about half a block away. I saw that it was Larry, the big guy with the trampy girlfriend. He was sneaking up in the shadows, careful to make sure that Bruce didn't see him. All of the sudden, like a cat attacking a bird he has stalked, Larry struck and struck fast. He ran across the street and before Bruce had a chance to react, Larry shoved Bruce off the concrete wall and at least forty feet down to the pavement below. Then he turned and ran off, like no one saw him. That's how retribution was around here. Some guys, Bruce for instance, will go through life pulling some fucked up shit, all the while thinking it's a big city and it'll never catch up with them. It always eventually catches up with them though. Bruce survived the fall, but I bet he'll always remember Larry, and I doubt he'll ever sit up on that wall again. Hell, after that, I wouldn't sit up there either. That's a long, nasty fall. Can you believe that's not even the worst thing that happened to him?

Bruce was one of those people who seemed to be in the wrong place at exactly the right time. He had a girlfriend named Barbara who was always running around with someone else. Every time I saw her she was in a big hurry, with a different guy in tow. Just like clockwork, ten minutes later Bruce would show up, in search of her. He always seemed to appear just ten minutes behind.

One day Bruce and Barbara decided they'd had enough of the crazy San Francisco City life and drove to Oregon.

Barbara had family there, so it was somewhere to run away to. They went there hoping that just by moving away from the drugs everything else in life would be better. Well, it only took Bruce four weeks to decide that Oregon wasn't where he wanted to be. Barbara's little brother also decided he was going to leave as well. So these two knuckleheads, Bruce and Barbara's brother devised a brilliant plan of stealing a car and driving it to San Francisco; sounded like trouble in the making.

They found an unlocked, older model car and with a dent-puller, jerked the ignition out of the steering column. Then when Bruce put the ignition back into the steering column and turned it like there was a key in it, the car started right up.

Ok, that was step one of the plan. The next step was to steal license plates off of another car, so if the police ran the plates the car wouldn't come back as stolen. It didn't take very long to find another car of the same make and model. They switched the license plates thinking that nobody would have figured anything out by the time they got to San Francisco. Once in the city a car is pretty useless, so they didn't plan to keep it much longer.

Along the drive back, they saw a car, also the same type, parked on the side of the road. They figured since this trick worked once, it would work again. So they pulled up behind it and switched plates again. Bruce also decided to check the car door and found it unlocked. He climbed in and looked around looking for anything worth money or that just caught his eye. He checked out the glove box, under the seats, all over the car but only found a couple of cassette tapes that he took. They got to the city and got rid of the car within a week. That was the last Bruce thought about it until about three weeks later.

I ran into Barbara (who managed to find her own way back) and she was crying. She said, "The cops kicked in the door this morning, a whole bunch of them! They came in with their guns drawn and arrested Bruce. There was dope and paraphernalia all over the place, but they said they were homicide officers and weren't here for the drugs!" That's about all they said to her and just left with Bruce. Barbara was really shook up about the whole thing and needed to get out of the hotel. She had grabbed all the drugs and left. That was when I ran into her.

I went to see Bruce that weekend and I didn't recognize him; he had shaved his head completely bald and he had a crazed look in his eyes, like a trapped, wild animal.

He sat down on his side of the window and picked up the other telephone handset and told me what happened.

The last car that they pulled up behind and switched plates with was the missing car of one of the 'Night Stalkers' victims. They had Bruce's fingerprints all over the interior and he was going to be charged with murder for all of the Night Stalkers murders.

Bruce had had a complete mental collapse and I can't really say I blame him. I don't know exactly how I'd react to that kind of situation either. They eventually caught the real 'Night Stalker' and released Bruce from jail. Bruce continues to shave his head. To say the least he was never quite the same happy crazy self again, but a whole lot more serious. To be told that you are in jail for murder and going to be tried for something that you didn't do can do permanent damage to a guy.

There's no telling where or when the retribution may come, so I made it a point to try to make as few enemies as possible. I let Stan do that; he seemed to like making enemies. He had a little of that bully quality that I admired through high school. I doubt I could ever be a bully myself, I guess from actually being on the bullied side of the whole game. But I could stand back and observe the bullying, just to critique it later and help develop Stan into a much better thug. He was a big guy, but he needed a little push in the right direction before he began to instill fear in others. After a while, he got pretty good at making other people feel uncomfortable. I sort of showed him that since he now had the bag, he didn't have to be as nice. If someone owed us money, I'd pump Stan up to do something about it. It wasn't really that hard; he had some anger issues to begin with. Don't we all?

It was pretty funny the way I had the whole plan set up. Stan would terrorize anyone who owed us money, while I seemed to be the only one who had any control over him. They would think Stan was the bad guy and I was the good guy. They would even sneak up to me when Stan wasn't around and ask if I could try to talk some sense into Stan, calm him down, make him understand that they will have his money to him in no time. Little did they know that I was the guy who was pulling Stan's chain. I was the guy getting him all pumped up. They were asking the wrong guy for help. Of course I never said that, I made it out like I was the only way they were going to get out of this trouble. That really paid off later on down the line, when Stan and I parted ways. Everyone preferred to deal with me instead of going through that maniac, Stan.

During our short period of learning to be drug dealers, we met another freak who shared our views. You couldn't miss this guy in a crowd. I guess the Mohawk gave him away. It stood a little less than two feet off the top of his head, and he liked to paint it different colors. Needless to say, we began calling him Mohawk John.
Another John in this whacked out world of meth. I met a lot of Johns and a lot of Tonys throughout this whole ordeal, so I gave most of them nicknames, to avoid

getting them all confused.

Mohawk John and I hit it off from the beginning. He was the one that started planting the seed that Stan was taking advantage of me. When I look back in retrospect, I can see the ulterior motives behind this. John didn't like the partnership Stan and I had, and he wanted his share of the pie, so to speak. John would point out how I was the one making money, while Stan just used it or gave it away. After a while, it began to become clear that this was an unbalanced partnership we had. I was doing more, selling more, dealing more than Stan. But I wasn't getting ripped off. Stan was very good for that. After talking to John for a while, I knew I had to go out on my own. I got tired of splitting the profits that I felt I created. It was time for me to spread my wings and fly. But I had to do it in a way that I didn't make an enemy of Stan. That would turn out to be harder than it looked.

Mohawk John told me, "Yeah, I'm going down to LA for a while, near the beach. You ever heard of Venice Beach?"

I said, "I lived down in Hollywood for a short while, but I can honestly say that I never went near the ocean while I was down there. Where are you going? What's the plan?"

He said, "I've been down there once before, and there are beautiful girls everywhere, as well as a crowd like the people we know up here. I'm just tired of San Francisco and I want a change." It didn't take much convincing to talk me into it. I needed something else anyway. This was getting a little boring, and I still felt like I was being used by Stan.

The next day I decided to broach the subject with Stan. He got pissed off at first, thinking it was just an excuse to bail on him (which it was), but I knew how to worm my way out of that. I had always known that Stan would never leave San Francisco. He was stuck there, with no desire to ever change. So I twisted that around and said, "Actually, I was hoping that you'd come along. It would be harder to hitch a ride with three people but we could manage."

He reacted just as I thought he would and said, "I've got to stay here, I have an appointment next week and I'm waiting for a check to come in the mail." So there was my way out, without making an enemy. I just played on that and left the window open that I might be back and we may be back in business again. That was enough for him, so I just left it at that.
I knew that would never happen, but at least I didn't make an enemy. I ended up with enough of them without even trying.

CHAPTER 6
BACK TO L.A. (YOU GOTTA BE KIDDING!)

Mohawk John and I headed up to the freeway onramp and within fifteen minutes had a ride out of San Francisco. I never thought I'd be headed back to L.A. It just always left an awful taste in my mouth. The people there were stuck-up and very me oriented. At least the people I had met so far, and my world of friends weren't a great group to compare to.

This ride got us down past San Jose, and pretty close to Santa Cruz. We were gonna head to Santa Cruz and kick it there for the night, so we stuck out our thumbs again, and hoped for a quick ride. A red convertible mustang pulled up and it contained two beautiful blonde college students. The one in the passenger side said, "Hey, need a ride? And nice Mohawk!"

Like a flash we were off again. As we drove down the road we discovered that they were UCLA college students who drove up to San Francisco for a weekend. They were on their way back to Venice. What luck, we found a ride all the way there. By the time we passed through San Luis Obispo (about half way), they had told us their whole story. There was another one of them that couldn't make the little road trip with them, but we'd meet her shortly. They were all enrolled in UCLA and their fathers had gone in together to rent this condo for the three of them right down near Venice Beach. They said it was a huge place and we were welcome to stay for a while. We didn't know just what that offer included, but when we discovered, it included a lot of fringe benefits.

When we arrived in Venice, we went straight to their condo to meet up with their other roommate. They actually all looked like they were related. All three were blonde, blue-eyed California girls who spent a lot of time in thong bikinis down on Muscle Beach. They had perfect tans from being out in the sun all the time. That's all right, I had a pretty good tan before long myself.

After going to the Davy Jones Liquor Locker to get some beer, we all went up in the condo so they could show us around. We had a few beers each and then things were all laid out on the table, so to speak. The two beauties that gave us a ride asked if we were ready for bed, but it was obvious that they weren't talking about sleep. We were all for it and so the night was terrific. I can't even give you these girls names, because I don't really remember who was who, although we lived there for three months. I just remember that we didn't always go to bed with the same person. Once in a while we didn't go to bed with just one either. They were really freaky and I had a suspicion that they had planned this out in advance, and also that we weren't the first.

They never mentioned it, but they were just way too relaxed about it. There was never an uncomfortable time at the beginning for them, just for me and John. But after a few days of this, we became very comfortable with it.

It lasted for three months, and then one day two of the girls told me that they wanted John to leave. John can be a little on the crazy side, the Mohawk can attest to that. They were starting to feel a little uncomfortable around him so they needed him to go. It wasn't a tough decision for me. I came down here with John and we were going to stay together in this insanity down in L.A. So I told them that I would be going with him. They didn't really protest, maybe the fun and games were over for them. They had definitely lost a lot of the thrill for me. I had been meeting other girls around the beach and I wasn't even there that often anymore. I had left John there though, and I bet that's when he started to get to them.

So we went up the beach about a mile or two until we got to Santa Monica, the next town north. They had a pier there that was like L.A.'s version of the Civic Center Plaza. Lots of tourists during the day and during the night, there was a whole different world, one that the tourists weren't quite as safe in.

John and I found a place to buy pot, a place to sell pot, and a place to hide with our pot. That's just about all we needed to get started. After a week or two we had enough money to rent a motel room somewhere, but we had discovered 'squatting.' 'Squatting" was the in thing down there. We knew people who held full time jobs, yet still preferred to squat somewhere rather than pay rent to someone. When you squatted, you found an abandoned building, found your own creative and secret way in, and just lived there rent free. With as many squatters as there were, the odds of you finding a place all to yourself were slim. So you shared buildings with other squatters, but there was an unwritten code about staying out of the other peoples' areas. When someone breaks that code they are usually punished by eviction from a house that we don't even really have any say about. Who are we to eject someone when we are staying there illegally?

But you had to have these rules because there was an occasional theft in the area. When you already have nothing, and someone else has something you want, it can be very tempting. It's not like they can go out and buy it themselves. I noticed that in these groups, there was always someone talking about how things would be if they were rich. They say money doesn't make the world go around, but try telling that to the poor. Being rich was a main topic of discussion for us. What we would buy, what we would eat, and where we would live. There were a few older people in this Santa Monica world, but it was mainly comprised of young adults and teenagers.

It was almost like "Lord of the Flies." Sitting in an abandoned building, making up our own rules, and trying not to follow any of the past ones that we felt were unfair. It was us against the whole world and we had no proper guidance. Most of the people I met hadn't had proper guidance their entire life.

When you were too poor to afford the extremely high housing costs, you either applied for government assistance, which houses you in the low, low-income fleabag hotels, or you take the homeless route. A few of the people I met in Venice/ Santa Monica had permanent residences but most received their mail at a post office box or general delivery at the Post Office because they had no permanent address. They lived on the streets.

Living on the streets didn't mean living out on the streets, but living and sleeping in any available, hidden away place that I felt comfortable enough about not being disturbed when I slept. During the normal travels of the day, I was constantly on the look out for a new 'squat.' I always had a list of possible squats, just in case I have to leave the one I was living in quickly. If the cops, fire department, or anyone who looks like the owner of the building comes snooping around, it's time to vacate and find new dwellings. The list came in very handy. I didn't have a lot of possessions, but I did have a small bag of clothes and showering necessities. I didn't want to have to carry it all around with me all day while I looked for a new 'squat,' so it was important to always have a plan of escape. I usually moved in a hurry.

It didn't take long for John and I to uncover the second world on, under and around the Santa Monica Pier in a three block long park. We found the usual scattering of bag ladies, winos, and crazies as well as the pimps, hookers, drug dealers, and drug addicts. The Santa Monica Pier was their home and they seldom left the three-block area unless it was to find drugs unavailable at the pier or the need to be present for their government assistance meeting, maybe to pick up their bi-weekly check. Otherwise, the pier was their roost and they knew everything that was going on around their pier. Things that would make a tourist never want to come back and visit.

Drug deals were going on everywhere, either between pier folk and tourists or just between us. Low-grade marijuana was the main commodity, but a few deals for stronger drugs were always available. I only dealt in pot, I hadn't been exposed to the harder drugs enough yet to dabble in selling anything heavier than pot. It was easy to come by, not too expensive, and if done properly, I could double my money. 'Doing it properly' entailed not smoking, giving away or just fucking off my profits. 'Doing it properly' didn't happen very often. I possessed a knack of doing all three of the major no-no's, mainly the fucking off part.
I liked to share the wealth, but I always made sure I had my re-up money first. I

made back what I spent and had the same amount for the next time before I started playing around and spending money.

Finding pot in large quantities that I could break down into smaller quantities for resale was easy enough, once I learned the method. I had some money in my pocket, so I asked one of the local pot dealers where I could find something larger than the dime bags (10 dollar bags) that he was selling. He said that he had just sold his last bag and was getting ready to go re-up and I was welcome to tag along if I wanted, as long as I didn't act like a moron.

We took a bus ride to Pico Blvd., deep into a Hispanic neighborhood. Many of the people who live there don't speak a word of English. Why should they? Their community is immense and anyone that they need to converse with speaks Spanish. The Department of Motor Vehicles even offers the written part of the driver's license test in Spanish. In San Francisco, they offer the test in Spanish and Chinese, but I have yet to see any street signs in either of those languages.

We exited the bus at Pico Blvd onto a street crowded with young Mexican males, all standing around in small groups, looking bored and suspicious. I know that a majority of these guys came from countries other than Mexico, but I'll just call them Mexicans for this story to avoid having to list each and every nationality. I spotted a few white guys here and there, but they didn't stand very long in the group before they were off on their merry way.

I was about to ask my friend a few questions about the whole situation, but realized that the best way to learn the routine was by just following this guy while he purchased his pot. I asked him to tell me the prices I would expect to pay for certain amounts; after that, I kept my mouth shut and watched.

He said, "They have a very specific way to sell. Although it may look like they are going to rip you off, they aren't. This is the way that they feel safest dealing drugs out here. They won't rip you off, it's a machismo thing. They have too much pride to rip you off. Everyone here knows everyone else and they are proud of the money making business that they have and they don't want any kind of bad reputation. Just do it exactly the way they tell you and you'll get your pot. Try to rip one of them off and the whole block kicks your ass."

I don't know if the whole machismo story was bullshit, but from my dealing on Pico, I've never had a bad experience, except for the day that the cops raided. I'll get back to that.

He walked past a few groups of Mexicans, some asking "What's up?" or saying something in Spanish that I couldn't understand. I assumed that they were saying, "What's up?" in Spanish. I could tell that he was heading for a specific group and when we walked up, one of the Mexicans stepped out and shook his hand as though he knew him. I soon discovered that if you are a steady customer to one specific guy, he will give you deals and lower the price a bit. They like the constant, repeat business.

The guy that I was following spoke Spanish, so I couldn't understand what they were saying. I didn't need to understand the words, as long as I understood what was going on. They agreed on a price and he gave the Mexican his money. We turned and walked away. He told me to follow him and we walked half way down the block to an alley. There were a few garbage dumpsters in a row, lined up against the wall. He went over to one of the dumpsters and reached his hand into one of the square metal holes, where the garbage truck's forks lifts the dumpster to deposit it's contents into it's belly. He pulled out a big bag of weed and we started to leave the alley, heading back to Pico and the bus stop heading home to the pier. I stole a glance into the other square holes and there were bags of pot in each hole.

He saw me glancing into a hole and muttered, "Remember the whole block of ass kickings?"

I understood what he meant and didn't say anything back to him. I moved a little farther away from the row of dumpsters though.

I wandered around on Pico for a few minutes, then up to a group of Mexicans. I didn't know one from another, so I went to the one that I knew I could remember and recognize the next time I came to re-up. A lot of them looked similar but I eventually found a guy that was shaven completely bald and had a huge diamond in one of his ears. He possessed the tiniest ears I've ever seen on a full-grown human's head. He was less than five feet tall, so you make the call on whether or not he was full grown. I knew that I wouldn't forget this guy.

'Ears,' as he was fondly referred to by my friends and me, looked up when I walked up to him. I asked, "Do you know where I can find some pot?"

He asked, "How much?"

I replied, " I have a hundred dollars. What can one hundred bucks get me?" He laughed and said, "Enough to get you stoned for a long time."

I gave him my money and he told me to go over to a flower box, next to a building stoop down the block. When I got to the box, I couldn't find the pot. I searched it completely; you never knew how well it might have been hidden.

With no discovery after a complete search of the flower box, I went back to talk to 'Ears.' I told him, "I checked the flower box, but I couldn't find anything there. I looked pretty good."

He said something to his friend and his friend ran off. He ran to the flower box for a brief second, into the building that the flower box belonged to, and back out on the street in just a few seconds more. He came back over to our group, said something to Ears in Spanish and handed him a baggie.

Ears handed me the baggie and said, " Sorry, my mistake." He reached down into the crotch of his pants and pulled out another bag of pot. After shoving his hand into the baggie and pulling out a handful of pot, he gave me the pot. I wasn't sure why he handed me the pot, so I just thanked him.

He said, "Sorry, my mistake." Ears was a man of few words, I think that he didn't know a lot of English. He was a good person to know and he took really good care of me, each and every time I went to see him.

I took the pot that Ears gave me and added it to the bag. I went back to the pier and sold two hundred and twenty dollars worth of pot while I screwed off the rest. This was the start of another path that ended badly.

By the way, I went down to Pico Blvd one day and LAPD had all of the Mexicans sitting in a row on the curb of the street. Immigration Services were there as well, finding guys that were in the country illegally. There were cops everywhere, so I walked straight across the street to the opposing bus stop, and caught the next bus headed back towards the pier. That was the only bad experience I ever had on Pico and it wasn't so bad for me; it was bad for the Mexicans.

The first thing that I did after I sold about two hundred dollars worth of pot, was to take John, me and three other pier folk out to dinner and then to rent a motel room. It was nice to rent a motel room once in a while, to sleep somewhere with a lock on the door and a shower. We usually swam in the Pacific Ocean at some point during each day, so showers weren't a main priority, but it was a pleasant luxury once in a while. As my mother use to tell me when I was a kid and hated taking baths, "A little soap never hurt anyone."

Motel rooms were a highlight, but were only afforded once or twice a week, on the other days, we squatted. Squatting was the normal, accepted form of protection from the elements as well as a place to lay my weary head at night. We always squatted in groups, for protection, as well as human company. If we came across other squatters, if they were in groups, we usually talked to them and asked if there was room for more squatters. It was hard for them to say no, since they were staying there illegally, as well. Whenever we came across a single, solitary squatter, there was usually a good reason that he was alone. Most of them are clinically insane and only care for their own company. We steered clear of those squats. Those were the squats that caught fire and burned to the ground.

We each had a bedroll consisting of a sleeping bag and a few blankets for padding when we slept. We also had one or two bags each of personal belongings. We traveled light. You decide to travel light after carrying your stuff around with you for a week or two. I didn't have a lot of possessions to begin with and I made sure not to collect too many more along the way. I would usually just replace whatever I lost or destroyed.

It started out with only John and me, but in days we met two young, female runaways and another teenage guy. I don't even remember the name of the guy, he only lasted three weeks before deciding that life on the streets wasn't for him. I met a few like him, all cut from the same expensive piece of silk. A rich kid who wasn't happy with his life and decided to try something new and different. A month of living on the streets is enough for them to make an educated decision to try something else. They always seemed to have a little money to contribute to the cause, probably more than they ever let on having. So, we were always willing to let them tag along. They would either run out of money or have a bad experience, call up Mom or Dad, and fly out on the next plane home. I often wonder what they took home from their lives on the streets. Did it help them make better choices in life? Did it affect where they planned to go with their lives? Or did they put that month into a little box and hide it away in the deep, forgotten parts of their memory, never to be thought about again? It would be a shame to think that the experience didn't change their lives for the better in some way.

The two girls were not in the same situation as the rich kid. They had only met recently and decided to travel together, but their lives seemed very similar. They were both sixteen and from broken homes that had a lot of weird shit going on with adult men in their lives. They both decided that life away from home would be much more pleasant and bearable than life at home, no matter what that life may be. They came from different states and had just met in California, but they had formed a close bond with one another.

Cindy had a punk rock look; spiked and red colored hair, a pierced nose, and purposely tattered clothing, but she possessed none of the punk rock attitude. She was quiet, shy, and apprehensive around most people, as a result of her tough childhood. Once she warmed up to you and felt comfortable, you couldn't shut her up. She was quite chatty and very funny, but she still held everyone at arms length, a form of self-protection. Kimi was the only person she ever let all the way in.

Kimi, with an "I", as she liked to say, was a short, overweight Asian girl with glasses who appeared as if she spent the majority of her life with her nose in a book. She had an opinion on everything and didn't really care to hear anyone else's opinion on anything. With all of her flaws, she truly loved Cindy and would have done anything for her. I thought Kimi liked Cindy a little more than Cindy appeared to realize or admitted to noticing. I even mentioned it to Cindy once in private, but she said that I was reading too much into it, that Kimi loved her like a sister.

I fell for Cindy the moment I met her. I was only 17/18 at the time, so her age wasn't a concern. I told myself that I could have just as easily left home at sixteen instead of seventeen. I talked to her within five minutes after I first saw her on the pier. I walked up and started talking to her, hoping to strike up a conversation. She stared at me for a second before turning one hundred and eighty degrees around on the beachside bench, to face away from me. She was sitting there all alone with a sad, far away look in her eyes. I thought she was going to cry. I hoped that making her laugh might help.

I reached into my pocket and pulled out a quarter. Then, like any teenage boy, I used probably the worst line in history. I said, " You look real sad, sitting here deep in thought. I was wondering what you were thinking. A quarter for your thoughts? You know, inflation and all."

As she continued to stare out at the ocean, I said, " I'm sorry if I bothered you. Sometimes, it just helps to have someone to talk to."

I went back over to where John was sitting on a blanket in the grass. He was in the middle of selling pot to someone when I walked up and sat down. I told him that the girl wouldn't even look at me, let alone speak to me. Maybe, she spoke a different language and couldn't understand me? That is a good possibility in California.

Five minutes later, her friend came strolling over to her with two sodas. I stood up and John asked where I was going. I told him to stay with the blanket and pot, that I would be right back.

I walked back over to the bench, with the quarter smartly tucked away in my pocket this time, and began talking to Cindy's friend. She was friendly and seemed to enjoy the conversation. I asked her why she was sitting on a bench on

Santa Monica Pier. She wasn't shy and answered every question I asked, even asking a few questions of her own about me. I talked to her for nearly fifteen minutes before she said, "Oh, this is my friend, Cindy. She's really shy and doesn't talk to very many people."

I said, "It's cool, sometimes it's better to be silent. When you aren't talking, you listen to much more, take in everything around you."

Kimi said, "But it's OK, I do enough talking for the both of us. By the way, my name is Kimi, with an I."

Whipping out my Dad's sense of humor, even at age 18, I said, "Then, wouldn't that make you, Kimi with two I's? K-I-M-I."

From the other side of Kimi, Cindy laughed and said, "I guess you are Kimi with two I's."

Being another visually challenged individual in this world, I said, "No, she's Kimi with four eyes and I'm Aaron with four eyes, since we both wear glasses."

She laughed and said, "Hi, I'm Cindy."

Cindy was never shy around me again. I don't think she ever told Kimi that I had come over earlier with the quarter. If she had, Kimi would have definitely mentioned that. That's the way Kimi was.

The group of us hung out all of the time, and were together the entire day, except when I went to re-up. I never took anyone else with me to go see 'Ears' because I didn't want to freak him out with a bunch of different people. Things were going good with 'Ears' and I didn't want things to change. He was always there when I looked for him and the prices went down, the more I bought. Things were running smoothly and I didn't want to create any waves. Don't try to fix what ain't broke, right?

The trips to see 'Ears' only took an hour and a half, three hours total if I went twice in one day. It was usually just once, early in the day, and by the end of the day, I'd have enough money to re-up the next day, plus extra spending money that always seemed to find a way to spend itself by morning, since there were four of us spending it. I know that at one point there were five of us in the group, but I don't remember enough of the rich kid to even include him in my story. A few nights after meeting the two girls, Cindy and I were walking alone, down on the beach. John and Kimi were off on separate tasks and neither would be back for a while. I listened to the roar of the surf, somewhere next to us, but enveloped in darkness. As we walked along, I looked at Cindy. I could see that she was deep in thought, far away, yet ready to snap back in case I said something that required a response. I wasn't about to say a word, I just walked next to her and watched her think.

Almost as if she were reading my mind, she stopped walking and turned to me. It took her a moment to work up the nerve to speak before she said, "If you are still willing to offer the quarter, I'll take it now."

I reached into my pocket, pulled out two quarters and put them in her hand. I said, "Hopefully, two quarters will buy me the complete story."

I took her other hand in mine and walked her over to a nearby bench. We sat down and she talked for nearly two hours. I don't feel comfortable ever revealing exactly what she talked about, but her childhood was one of the most tragic stories I've ever heard. She cried while she told me everything, like she needed to get this all off her chest. She needed someone to tell her that none of it was her fault that she didn't deserve anything that she went through and now that she is on her own, living as an adult, no one will ever be able to do anything like that to her, ever again.

I sat quietly next to her, wiping her tears away and just listening. I had a million things that I wanted to say, but I had finally been able to get her to open up to me. I didn't want to interrupt her and cause her to stop. While I sat silently listening, I would have cried if I had been able to. Writing about this now brings me close to tears and it was twenty years ago. When you hear a person's story, it becomes much easier to understand why he is the way he is.

Cindy and I became fast friends. Which seemed to upset Kimi. Kimi liked the fact that Cindy would only talk to her. She didn't like Cindy becoming friends with me. Cindy talked all of the time now and she was quite funny. She was able to see little things in life that no one else would ever notice. It's more proof that you notice more when you spend your life listening.

Sex with Cindy was more uncomfortable and awkward than beautiful and romantic. I had close to zero experience and she had way too much bad experience. We seemed to be more relaxed when we were just lying next to each other talking.

Now, whenever we walked around or sat on the grass, Cindy would hold my hand or sit close to me. Kimi was starting to get irritated and it showed. Sometimes Cindy would grab my hand, then grab Kimi's hand with her other. She and Kimi used to walk around a lot holding hands; it made Cindy feel safer.

It's hard to imagine how this little, terrified girl traveled across eight states by herself before she met Kimi.

Kimi would walk with us for a few minutes before she would let go of Cindy's hand and wander off a little to the side, looking at the landscape. I could tell by the way she walked away that it just wasn't the same when she was forced to share Cindy. After a few moments, she would stroll back like it was nothing, talking about her opinion on something. She had many opinions on just about everything. I noticed that she didn't take Cindy's hand, though.

It was like this for three weeks before Kimi could take it no more. She completely freaked out and trashed the squat. She threw everything that she could lift against the nearest wall, sometimes two walls. Then, as if she had practiced this many times at home as a child, she began screaming and crying uncontrollably. I had to listen to this for a good fifteen minutes before she finally calmed down enough for Cindy to attempt to talk to her.

Kimi said that she wanted to go home. Cindy started to cry, out of fear of losing her 'road-dog'. They were traveling together and she didn't want Kimi to desert her. Kimi said that her mind was made up. She was leaving now and Cindy had the choice, to either leave with her or stay at the squat.

Kimi was Cindy's travel partner and John and I were just two guys that she met along the way. I knew her answer long before it came out of her mouth, but I was surprised how long it took. She sat there thinking until Kimi was completely finished packing up her belongings, but she wouldn't look at me. When Kimi was completely finished packing, Cindy stood up, gave me a half smile and shrugged, before she began packing her things. She didn't say a word, just angrily stuffed her belongings into her bag and rolled up her bedroll.

When she was finished, she stood up and turned to me. She kissed me and said, "I love you." It was the first and only time I ever heard her say those words and I hope it will be the last memory I ever forget. She turned, gave Kimi a dirty look, picked up her things and walked out the door. I assumed Kimi was out the door right behind her, but I was too dazed to even see straight. It was the first time any woman looked me in the eyes and said, "I love you," and truly meant every word of it. It was a feeling like nothing I had ever experienced. Everything tingled and my ears started to ring. I felt something that I knew, no matter how many more times in my life I hear those words, it will never be enough. That feeling was more addictive than any of the multitudes of drugs I have tested. It was so intense that I can still feel it every time I hear it. When I feel it emanating from them, along with the words I know that to someone, I am very special. What a wonderful feeling!

Just like that, Cindy was gone. When you live on the street, people come and go from your life, here one day, gone the next. We never asked each other for last names. Our community was small enough that one name worked. I never knew Kimi or Cindy's last names and I think that those weren't even their real names. One night, Cindy and Kimi were arguing and Cindy called Kimi 'Patricia.' They walked away to finish their argument and when they returned, she was Kimi again. They never mentioned it, so neither did I.

I doubt I will ever see Cindy again and I can't help but wonder if she ever found the special someone that she needed to survive in her terrified life. I have my memories and that will have to do.

John and I were on our own again, but that didn't last very long. Since Kimi destroyed out squat and probably alerted the neighbors by her disturbance, John and I decided that it would be best if we vacated the premises immediately. We packed up whatever belongings that were still intact after the rampage and went to the next squat on my list.

We found a squat and shared it with two of the nicest skinheads you could ever meet. I know that sounds funny, but for being asshole skinheads, they knew who their friends were and stuck by them like glue. I really never saw them do or say anything against other races, and they would always talk badly about other skinheads. I guess, at least in their twisted view of life, there were two different types of skinheads, ones that hated every other race and ones who hated the establishment. These were establishment hating fellows and they definitely had a lot of hate built up. I saw them get into fights every day, mostly with people who hated skinheads and thought these guys were racists. They never tried to defend their beliefs, they just liked fighting, I'd assume.

For a couple weeks, we sat on the pier, John and I selling our wares while we watched the three or four skinheads play their little game (there was always a few more like minded fellows up on the pier hanging with our boys.) They would drink beer, play their loud, obnoxious music, and manage to get into fights. It was highly entertaining for a while. There was never a dull moment when these guys were around.

One day I asked our hairless friends if they wanted to partake under the pier.
Of course they did, we went down there often, either to smoke or take care of a transaction. We were standing in a circle smoking a joint when a guy walked right up to us and said, "Hey, I smell something I've been looking for all day."

John asked, "How much are you lookin' for? I got a couple dimes."

He replied, " Damn, after looking all day, I was hoping to get more than that."

John looked over at me, knowing that I had a lot of pot on me, but seeing that I was apprehensive about letting everyone know that. So I said, "How much are you willing to spend? We might be able to help you out, depending on how much."

The guy said, "Hold on a sec, let me check and see exactly how much I have."

This is the point of every drug transaction that made me the most nervous. This is the point that undercover would swoop in on you. This is the point where someone hands you a wad of cash and it's not always the right amount. And like in this instance, this is the point that someone would pull a gun out on you.

He pulled out one of those nickel-plated snub nosed jobbers, like you always see on T.V. In one of those tough guy voices said, "Why don't you give me all your pot and all your money?"

That's about all he got out when one of my skinhead friends, who happened to be nursing a forty-ounce bottle of Mickie's beer, clobbered him with the bottle. Before I knew it, one of the other fellows picked up the gun and threw it into the surf, way out in the water. At this point, it was time for action. We each took a shot at the guy, just for pulling a gun on us, but the skinheads continued the beating until John and I stopped them. They were pretty pissed off about having a gun pulled on them, what was someone thinking? Trying to rob a group of skinheads. We decided it was time to move and we went to the squat to regroup.

The next day went off without a hitch, everything as usual. Nothing happened for about three days; then they came and rounded us all up. We weren't too hard to find, a couple of long hairs who hung out with a couple skinheads. They picked us up all within two or so hours. I guess it took a few days for the guy to come out of his delirium to point a finger at who beat him up.

They threw all of us in the Santa Monica County Jail, each of us in their total of four jail cells. OK, maybe they had a few more, but not many. I don't remember much about the jail, mainly because the shock of L.A. County Jail has completely overlapped that small bit of my time in the system. I remember that the air conditioning was set real high, and that John and I were both in just shorts and sandals. It was freezing in there, but that was the least of my concerns. I also remember that breakfasts and lunches were frozen meals, microwaved lukewarm. To this day I think frozen breakfasts are a bad creation. I don't know exactly how they were intended to be heated, but not in a microwave. It makes everything taste just like everything else.

After two days of not hearing anything, just guessing what was going on between us, it was driving us nuts. We figured either we were in trouble for the squat, like maybe it burned down, or that the rumor about hidden cameras up on the pier was true, and we've been nailed for dealing. We never even gave the beat-up guy a second thought because why would he tell on us, if he had been trying to rob us. It's like when a hooker and some thug rob, 'roll,' some trick when his pants are down. Do you really think he's going to tell the police that he got robbed while he was getting a hummer from someone other than his wife? We figured he just wrote it up to experience, and wouldn't fuck with a group of skinheads again.

So when we finally went to court after our 72-hour waiting period, we went to court just to find out that we're all in for felony assault on a police officer. Oh great, here we go again. And this fucking guy was a bully too; I should have known. After we were escorted out of the courtroom and put back in the holding tank, a 'Public Pretender,' Public Defender came in and introduced himself. He told me that he was actually just my P.D. but that the other three attorneys weren't able to make it to their clients' hearing (I thought that was their job) and that the two Jewish lawyers were trying to have themselves removed from the case because they didn't want to defend skinheads.

He told me not to worry, that he had a plan. Actually, he was the best attorney I had throughout my whole gambit with jail. He gave me his card and said to call him collect the next day and we'd set up a regular schedule of calls to keep me informed. I called him the next day and he was actually there and accepted my call. He said that this whole case sounded really fishy and that he was going to get to the bottom of it. He stressed for me not to worry, that was until he found out they were sending us to LA County Jail to await our court hearings. He fought that, but the Santa Monica Jail said that they didn't have enough room to house us there, so off we went.

CHAPTER 7
DISCOVERING THE WORLD BEHIND THE WALLS

We were awakened at three-thirty in the morning to begin the long process of waiting to get on and off the bus bound for the county jail. The actual ride wasn't that long, it was being counted and re-counted before and after the ride. We all had heard the stories about the jail.

In the late eighties, this jail was on the news a lot for it's large population of gang bangers. This is where you heard the names of the crypts and bloods. I was never sure if it was crips or crypts or what, but I wasn't about to ask one of them. When I first came to LA originally, I was on the bus and made some comment about how this young black kid's pants were almost falling off. Before I knew it, I almost got beat up by a pack of thirteen year-olds. Luckily, there was a cop riding on the bus, and they knew better than to get the LAPD riled up.

The crypts wore blue and the bloods wore red, which wasn't really fair in jail because we all wore blue jeans. But the bloods managed to fly their colors, one way or another. You could always tell which side each one was on. When I went in there, LA county jail was a dangerous place, including the officers who ran it. They were as dangerous as they come. You could tell some of them were pumped up on steroids, by their massive size, short fuse, and insane behavior. They would constantly scream, " Nut to butt!!!!" which meant they wanted us single file, as close together as possible, walking down the hallways. It was a real zoo. I saw a lot of fights, but they were all squelched quickly by the large number of officers.

We were led shackled to each other through the jail to the reception area. That's where we got the customary strip search, gave up our street clothes, received linen, and sent our entire property home in a box, after they got to pick and choose through the contents. I've heard many stories about property never arriving to its destination; the cops considered all this stuff either bought illegally with drug money or stolen. So they took what they wanted.

After a few hours in there, where we were also given a bag with two slices of bread, a dried up piece of cheese, and a bruised apple. At this point, we hadn't eaten since 3:30 A.M., so we were willing to try it. You could tell the ones who'd been here before. They were the ones who were already wheeling and dealing their lunches for cigarettes. A cigarette was the last thing on my mind. I was beginning to feel that fucked feeling again. I didn't get shipped out there with John or the skinheads; they had a bunch of runs all day long from one jail to another, high output.

I was the only white guy on the bus. When we finished with all of this, we were then taken to sit in a line and wait to be fingerprinted and photographed. As we began sitting down along the wall of a long concrete hallway, a biker looking dude with a long beard and full sleeves of tattoos down both arms walked up to me. He shook my hand pulled out a full pack of cigarettes and split them with me. He said, " We gotta stick together in here, brother. We are now the minority and it isn't a pleasant place to be."

That was my first experience with the Aryan Brotherhood. They never pressured me into being part of their group, but if you wanted a place to feel a part of, they were willing to stand behind you. There were cliques in there just like anywhere else in life; the big difference was the respect thing. You were required to give respect to others in there. There was no fucking around about that. Lack of respect in there has ended many a life. You gave respect and you received respect, at least if they felt you deserved it. There was always a proving period, but I didn't really learn about any of that at first.

After we were photographed, we were being escorted down another long hall when one of these amped up officers pulled me out of line. "Come with me, " he said.

He walked me back down to where we were photo'd and I.D.'d and told me to walk over to some cop who was sitting at his desk doing paperwork. He said, "Just walk over there and stand in front of him and look at him. Don't say anything, just look at him. O.K.?"

Great, now they were playing games with one another and I was their toy. In the few hours I had been there, I had seen cops beat two different people. Not to say that they didn't deserve it, one of them surely did, but I just didn't want to be the third. I knew what they are capable of and what they can get away with. Like that prison here in California that arrested a group of officers for setting up fights between rival gangs and then betting on them. That would have never come to light if they wouldn't have video taped it and some disgruntled officer gave it to the press. That was just one prison out of thousands; what makes any of the other ones any different? They just don't tape it. There are plenty of lawsuits against different prisons and jails for improper treatment of prisoners, but you never hear of them in the press. A large percentage of the population thinks the prisoners deserve whatever they get in there, but I've seen someone come in for a petty theft of something from a store, and never leave. Where's the justice in that? Life for stealing a sandwich? They don't have any way to separate the real convicts from the one timers, so they just pile them in together. Putting them together just hardens the one timer and allows the convict to corrupt the mind and teach how to commit other criminal acts.

They want to show off about how much they know; they are actually training the rookies to be better criminals. We didn't have much else to do most of the time except talk.

So back to the desk of this cop. I walked up and just stood there, not saying a word. After a few seconds, he sensed that I was there and looked up. That's when the other cop yelled over, " Hey Joe, how'd this little fish get let loose in my pond?"

"Joe" looked me over and asked, " You ever been in jail before?"

I said, " No sir, this is my first time."

Joe said, " OK then, we're sending you to the softie dorm. We don't think you'll survive out on mainline, so we're sending you to a dorm full of guys like you."

Oh great, I wondered what "guys like me" meant. Well, I'd find out soon enough. All I could do was go with the flow. I didn't have much choice about where I went.

They took me up to one end of the jail, where they segregated the gays and the people they thought might not belong with the gangsters. They separated us from the gays, but they all had comments for the softie boys every time we walked by them for chow. That got real easy to ignore. I just looked forward and pretended they just didn't exist.

When I got to the dorm, I had to choose one of the top bunks because all of the bottom ones were occupied. It was obvious that a bottom bunk took some time to acquire. But I wasn't going to be there long enough to worry about a bunk. It was more like a sleep away camp than a jail. I have a feeling that this is what the juvenile system must have been like. There were different packs of people, who hung out together, while they picked on the small, lame, and weak.

After being there for two or three weeks, my attorney came to see me with good news. He had studied my case and had come to the conclusion that the police officer we beat up was acting outside the law. He was working without backup and he never announced he was a cop when he pulled out his gun. It was becoming obvious that this officer was intending to rob us, and that it had nothing to do with the law. At my next court hearing, he went into chambers with the judge, and when he came out, he said we would be released. My attorney told me to go into the courtroom, listen to what the judge had to say, and then thank him and get out of there.

When I went in before the judge, he looked really pissed off. You could tell that he didn't like to do this, but I was being held on trumped up charges, and he had to uphold the law. He made sure that I understood what was happening. He told me that I was to be released by the end of the day, and that I had twenty-four hours after that to get out of his county. He said I'd be re-arrested if I was found in LA county after tomorrow. Well, that settled that, I had to leave town. Of course I was released from the jail at ten minutes til midnight, but I didn't care. I was just glad to be out. I walked straight to the freeway, stuck out my thumb, and got the fuck out of Dodge. I knew when I wasn't wanted and that was all right with me; LA had lost its appeal after that little stint in their jail.

CHAPTER 8
BACK TO WHERE MY HEART BELONGS

The trip back to San Francisco was uneventful. That's exactly the way I wanted it, quiet, without any waves, just completely uneventful. When I got back to San Francisco, I headed to where I knew, the plaza. When I got there, it was as if I had never left. Two tweakers walked up and asked if I knew where they could score. I told them to give me an hour and I bet I'd have some. That was easy.

I saw someone I sold to before I left for LA. He had gone from the bottom tweaker just looking for a high, up the ladder to a dealer. I guess while I was gone, he met someone that helped him out. We went up and down the ladder pretty fast at times, which made the ride that much crazier. One minute you could be flat broke, the next day you might have a thousand dollars in your pocket. That's just about what happened to me. He asked that if he hooked me up with some dope, would I turn it over for him? The start I needed to begin my next run before a hard fall.

A little more than thirty hours later, I had a grand in my pocket and was high as a kite. Things were easier this time. I knew all the right people, I had customers from before that were very happy to see me back in SF, and I had a determination to make something this time. Although, this time it would be by myself, without a partner to feel like I'm always carrying. I went up that ladder, bottom to top, in no time. But, I did have a few slips.

I found myself using a few of Gary's old tactics to run my business, like having others sell my dope for me. It's impossible to be everywhere at the same time, so if I had it spread out, people selling it in different areas; all I had to do was go around and collect my money. So I bought a mountain bike. I rode a bike in the city for about two years, before I discovered the power and convenience of a motorcycle. Riding the mountain bike re-built my knee to the point of nearly one hundred percent. So I do have that to be thankful for.

One of the biggest problems with dealing was transporting large quantities without looking too suspicious. So we had to come up with really creative ways to smuggle it around, but make it accessible enough to give out during a transaction. I got really creative, using the seam of my pants, in the lining of my jacket, and even in a tennis ball with a slash in it, jammed in the spokes of my bike wheels. We had to keep it hidden, just in case we got 'jacked up' by the cops. Riding around on a bike at three in the morning is enough reason to get you jacked up. When you are high on meth, just looking spun-out is enough. I'd guess that I got jacked up about three times a month, but it came in spurts, like three times in one week.

They would pat you down, run your name for wants or warrants, and just hassle you about where you were going and what you were doing.

One night, just a few blocks away from the plaza, two of my cohorts and I were riding along the sidewalk when an undercover car pulled up on the walk in front of us. Out jumped two undercovers with badges pinned to their flannel shirts. One yelled, "Hey you."

It was obvious that he was talking to us, but we kept going without responding. That really pissed the bullies off. They walked up to us and pushed one of my 'friends' off his bike. He said, "Hey, I'm talking to you."

I said, "No you're not, you're pushing us around. What's your badge number?"

That really ticked them off; they could tell I was just being a smart-ass. This was before I realized just what these guys can get away with, and before I learned that respect thing. After learning that, even though you hate the cops, you still gotta respect their power. Not respect them personally, but respect the things they can and will do.

He walked up to me, "OK funny guy, climb down off that bike and let's talk. I want to see some ID and let me see that pack around your waist."

Uh-oh, that wasn't good. There was a big pouch in my pack that unzipped in the front, and was full of stuff like my wallet, keys, etc. There also was a small zipper in the back for the small rear pouch, which happened to be full of dope. As I climbed off the bike, I guess I wasn't moving fast enough, so without waiting for me to take the pack off, he reached forward, grabbed me by the pack, and pulled me to him. As I stood there he searched through the front of the pack, while it was still around my waist, never realizing there was a pocket in the back. You could tell he was really disappointed not to find anything on any of us. Just as they were letting us go, one said to the other, "Oh yeah, don't forget what that tweaker told us yesterday, check the tennis balls on the bikes."

Wow, now that wasn't cool at all. Fortunately, I stopped putting it in there just the day before, so we all had empty tennis balls. But that meant that someone told on us. By the end of all this, you come to find out that almost everyone is telling on you. It's surprising what some of these people would do to avoid any time in jail. They would put three other people in jail, rather than have to go themselves.

But it always caught up with them in the end. First, paperwork would circulate around. Official looking documents that would incriminate the person of something like informing or setting someone up to come in contact with the police. I'd hear about it from different people, ones who didn't know each other. Next, you'd just never see that person again. Everyone would speculate, but anyone who knew for sure wasn't talking. Maybe they heard about the rumor spreading like wildfire and got out of Dodge right quick. Who knows for sure?

Another close call, one of the many I had before it all came crashing down. I got away with all this for a while, but eventually you know that it has to catch up with you. Close calls can be as scary as actually getting busted. Especially when you come to the realization that the police department isn't to be fucked around with.

One day, early in the afternoon, I had just finished selling everything I had and it was time to "re-up." You can probably figure out what that means. It's time to go see the dope man. I hated this part the most. It's when you have the most on you. Plus you have to go deal with some hard core dope fiend who has all the power over you since he has the dope. You have to pretend to like him, even if he is the weirdest person you've ever met. Some of these freaks can't even go out in public because they are just too obvious in their own special way. Re-upping is the worst time to get jacked up by the police, but it always seemed to happen that way. I was walking down the street with three other people. Two guys that did a lot of running for me, and one of the girls I was running around with at the time. I never really had anything to compare to a girlfriend until the very end. It's probably the only thing that pulled me out of the morass I called life. I was caught in a whirlpool, with no way out, and one woman managed to pull me out of that. That's later on, I'm jumping way ahead of myself. Back to the street with my three friends.

We were walking along, enjoying the sunshine, and talking about who was going to go with me. I wanted one of the guys to go, because if I didn't have to carry it, I wasn't going to. It's amazing to look back now and see how someone was willing to carry all that dope, just with the promise that you'll get him high afterwards. They would commit a felony for less than twenty dollars. After the first time I was arrested by the police, I always looked at it like that. If you are going to commit a felony, you better get paid well for it. We didn't even see the two undercovers walk up to us.

The officers walked up to both sides of me, sandwiching me between them. They told us to stand up against the wall. We were standing there, out in public, with people walking by watching the action unfold.
The cops were going through our pockets looking for anything that they could arrest us for. After searching all four of us and creating a huge scene, they

climbed back into their undercover cop car and drove off very quickly. We were still in shock from the close call and hadn't realized the full aspect of what had happened yet. It was when we started looking for the money that it all started to become clear. None of us had it and those cops ran off really quickly. I said we should go back to my room and figure out what we can do about this. We can't just keep standing out here on the street with everyone looking at us and pointing. I felt really vulnerable standing outside in the open.

My hotel was a seedy looking, Hindu owned, roach infested, poor excuse for a place to stay. I could have afforded better, but I wanted to stay in an area where I blended in. This was a building full of prostitutes, drag queens, dope dealers, and others with serious mental issues, the perfect place for me. After a year or two of living in these hotels I realized that I wasn't blending in well at all. Every person that saw me there knew instantly why I was there and what I was up to. After being robbed, it became quite apparent that I needed to move to a more respectable location if I wanted that feeling of safety and security again.

We walked up to the front desk and requested to be buzzed in by Mr. Patel, the Hindu slumlord who owned the place. It was strange that at every single hotel I rented a room, the hotel proprietor was named Mr. Patel. For a while, I just assumed that they were all related to each other. After a few years someone clued me in that Patel meant hotel manager. That explained a lot. They always lived in the hotel room closest to the office and it was always full of people. They never seemed to sleep and there was always a weird smell coming from their room, a very strong curry smell and something else that I've never been able to pinpoint.

By the time we got up to the room, I had worked myself up to a good fury. How dare the cops take my money! Who do they think they are? We weren't doing anything wrong, just walking down the street minding our own business. I didn't stop to think of a reason for me to be carrying four thousand dollars in cash or what had happened to me in Missouri with the police. I felt as if I had been robbed and I wanted to get some kind of payback. So I did probably the stupidest thing I could possibly do, I called the police department and asked to speak to a supervisor. Who knows if they ever actually let me talk to one, but the person I talked to sounded very sympathetic. After I told him what happened, he said that he knew exactly which officers did that and that they were already being investigated for other reasons. He said that he would send down two officers to take my statement and it was very important that I follow up with this, that they couldn't take care of this if the victim didn't step forward. I fell for this bullshit hook, line, and sinker. He sounded so sincere.
I hung up the pay phone and went back upstairs to wait for these officers to come. Alan and Skeeter, the two guys with me at the time, were waiting upstairs

with Renee. Alan was a skinny little tweaker who wore a black beret and combat boots all the time to look a lot tougher than we all knew he was. Skeeter was a six foot seven inch corn-fed hillbilly from Arkansas or somewhere. He wasn't much tougher than Alan but at least he looked the part. I've seen people cow down to him just because of the size difference. When I told them about the phone call, Alan suddenly had somewhere important to be. He said that he had to go and high tailed it out of there. He'd obviously seen enough of police officers for one day.

Well, you probably saw this coming, but believe it or not, I honestly didn't. When there was finally a pounding on my hotel door, I opened it to discover that the two officers who were sent here were the same two from earlier that day. Now, I began to realize that I might be in deep shit. They walked into my room, grabbed Skeeter by the back of his neck, gave him a pretty good smack and walked out into the hallway with him. After what seemed to be forever but couldn't have been more than five minutes, they came back in with Skeeter, who looked a little worse for wear, and pointed at me and asked me to follow them. We went down the hall to the stairwell where we would have a little more privacy. That's where they broke it down to me.

After pushing me up against the wall, they explained in no uncertain terms that they could do just about anything they wanted to, and if I had a problem with it, I could very easily be found floating in the bay. Just another dead dope fiend that no one gave a shit about and good riddance to bad rubbish was how they put it. I'll never forget the floating in the bay comment or the bad rubbish crack. Sometimes the weirdest things stick in your memory, some very inconsequential stuff that never seems to go away. That's what a lot of this book is about. Maybe if I write it all down, some of this little stuff will stop haunting my thoughts. What good is it, remembering a cop threatening to dump your body in the San Francisco bay? They never hit me, but they kept slamming me up against the cinder block wall, each time they wanted to make a point. Their points were well taken. That's when I knew to be very afraid of these guys. Not just these two, but all of them, because you never know if they are all working together. Every one of them that I've had contact with has been. It's only going by my experiences, but what else do I have to go by?

They left me there in the stairwell; their job was done. When I got back to my room, Skeeter was long gone and Renee was sitting there waiting to see if I was coming back at all or if they took me off to jail. Skeeter and I really never talked about what the cops said to us, I guess we both just assumed that we were told the same thing.
But, it was just another lesson in life that I would have not learned anywhere else. Learning to watch my back came easy for me. All those years in school

taught me well, and I was just applying what I had previously learned.

Sometimes, no amount of carefulness can protect you. Sometimes things happen just because someone else did something and the domino effect got you caught up in it. I was up in an apartment with my friend Muriah. He had gotten a settlement check and asked if I could come over and see him. When I got there, it was full of tweakers. Muriah had just bought a mountain bike, and in his crazed state of mind, decided he wanted to paint it a new color. So he went to Walgreens and bought thirty jars of nail polish and began painting the bike with the little tiny brush that came with each bottle. There were other people there as well. I always got uncomfortable when someone invited me over, and when I got there, the house was full of people. Some people will do anything for dope, so the fewer people the better and safer I felt.

When I came in, I knew it was a bad situation, and I needed to go quickly. I knew how much dope he wanted and that is all the dope I brought with me. As soon as I walked into the place, I pulled him into the bedroom and got my money and got rid of the drugs I was carrying. After that, I felt a little more comfortable. I didn't have anything anyone could try to take from me now. So I just hung out for a bit before deciding to go home.

There were other people in the apartment too, people I didn't know and people I really didn't care to meet. There was a girl there that looked about fifteen years old. That may have seemed young to some, but I was only eighteen myself, so who was I to judge? But this girl was very, very high. When I first arrived at the apartment, she was cleaning a bag full of junk jewelry. Little treasures to keep her entertained, I assumed. When I went into the bedroom with my friend, she asked him if she could use the phone. Muriah said sure, go ahead, just no long distance.

When I came out of the bedroom, she told us that she was going to call information for a phone number, but instead of dialing 4-1-1 she dialed 9-1-1. I asked her what she did then. She said she got scared and hung up; she didn't want to talk to any cop. I told Muriah that I had to go and I'd call him, but to be careful of this one; she's very flaky and could get him in trouble. When I called Muriah the next day, he had a very animated story about how the police showed up at his house because they were concerned that something was wrong due to the fact that someone called 9-1-1 and hung up. They were sent to investigate the call and find out if everything was OK. The police asked to see everyone's ID and when the girl showed her ID to them, they saw that she was under age and took her away.
I laughed and told Muriah, well, that was the easy way to get rid of her. I bet she wouldn't have just left if you had told her to go. She seemed to be making

herself at home there and didn't seem to have any plans to leave. He also said that he freaked out when he saw the cops at the door and flushed all the dope down the toilet, thinking it was a raid. So, of course I had to re-supply him. I told him that I didn't feel comfortable going there right now, but I'd meet him somewhere else. He understood my concerns and met me at a mutual friend's place. Muriah is another of the many people I met along the way that I don't have a clue whatever happened to him.

CHAPTER 9
THE CIVIC CENTER

I spent much of my time at the Civic Center. It was a centralized location that had thousands of tourists passing through it each day. I would run into about thirty people a day that I knew, some of whom I pretended not to know. When I heard someone screaming my name across the plaza, I'd turn and head the other way. I usually had drugs in my possession, so anytime someone would 'Front me off' (for instance, screaming my name out loud in a large group of people), it was time for me to go. It was hard enough trying to conceal the fact that I was trying to pass bags of drugs and money to people out in public so any added attention created by a spun-out, dope fiend was attention that I didn't need.

It was bad enough that they look completely disheveled, hair all messed up and unwashed, clothes dirty and torn only half of their shirt is tucked in (like they forgot what they were doing half way through tucking it in, or got side tracked because they were trying to do twenty things at once.) Dirty greasy hands from working on their mountain bike all day and night, non-stop, and sometimes with mismatched shoes or even one missing. You never really knew what kind of condition they would be in when you ran into them, based mainly on the amount of dope they'd done previously in the day. A large amount of meth gets a guy so wired up and energized that he starts to sweat. So it wasn't too surprising to see one or two guys a night, running around without shirts on at 2:00 A.M. in fifty-degree weather. Cruising around on stolen mountain bikes, they were soaked with sweat, eyes wide open and obviously spun out of their gourds. Its truly amazing how happy they can look: like they are having the times of their lives without a care in the world, at least until they come down, run out of dope and money and, worst of all, begin to feel tired and hungry. At that point they hate life and the only important thing on their minds is where they will get their next fix and what they will have to do to get the money to buy it. Food will come along whenever it comes along, but the important thing was finding the fix.

Once you do that either you'll find food or you'll get so spun that you aren't hungry anymore and just forget to eat. The search for dope seemed to be a constant project. There wasn't a real end steady supply from anywhere. You could get from a guy one day, but the next day, he might be out of dope, 'just got robbed,' selling really crappy dope this time, or even busted by the police and out of the game for a while. So most people had little books with lists of all the possible people to call when they were in search of a high. Each person had his own little codes and symbols that only he understood, for those times when they were 'jacked-up' by the police. The cops always looked through your address book to see if there were any names they recognized.

Then, just to be an asshole, the next time they ran into that person, they mentioned your name in hope of stirring up trouble or making you seem like a snitch. Another reason why so many people went by fake names in this tiny world I lived in.

People tried to stay anonymous, but at the same time they had to have a recognizable name for other tweakers. I didn't really care if anyone knew my name, but very few knew my last name. It was either: the kid, honest Aaron, or longhaired Aaron. There weren't a lot of other Aarons around, so no need to use a last name. It afforded you a little more protection and anonymity when you were running around in that life, but at the same time, it made it hard to write to someone when he got busted and sent to jail. Eventually, they all did. It was just another dangerous trap we dodged each day out there. Sooner or later one of those traps was going get you.

When you were arrested, you did your time and came back out hoping to be able to pick up right where you left off. Unfortunately most of everything you had before was now gone and you had to start anew. There were plenty of tweaker 'friends' around to get you high for your first time since freedom, as well as being there with their ideas of how you can 'come-up' from the nothing you had now. It always involved something illegal, so many people ended up back in jail in no time at all. It was a revolving cycle we got trapped into, with very few real ways out

Very few of the people I met had any family to speak of. Either they were all alone in the world or they had troubled their families to the point of them being disowned or like in my case, you disowned your family out of embarrassment of the condition you were in. I just felt that it was better not to involve my family in all of this shit.

Without family support behind a person, the only other way out was jail, drug programs, or assisted-living programs because of some devastating injury, or the ultimate ending, death; Not a lot of good choices out there.

Jail doesn't really do much but give you a chance to sit around with other 'like-minded criminals' and plan new ways to 'come up' once you got out. There really wasn't any kind of support in jail to help get clean or get a job. It was just a huge cattle farm. They herded us to and from different areas of the prison, too busy keeping the real troublemakers in line to spend time trying to help people change their lives.

Drug programs seem to have their hearts in the right place, but there are down sides to them as well. Some programs can be very strict and even verbally abusive. Others think that with the power of a large group of people, they can pressure someone into staying clean and sober. Those programs worked a little better, a littler higher success rate, but the temptation to get high can be very powerful at times.

People stay in the programs until they can't stand being yelled at anymore, can't handle the restrictive environments or just can't resist the urge to get high. The percentage of people making it all the way through a program their first time is pretty low, when you take out the ones sentenced from jail to serve in a drug program. Surprising how well a three to seven year suspended sentence can drive a person to complete a six to nine month drug program. But when you are talking about a junkie just walking in off the street wanting to be clean, not very many of them stay in for more than a week the first time. After the first time, the percentage goes up mainly because the addict is even more tired of his miserable life and tired of the constant run. They also know exactly what they are getting themselves into this time. Drug programs are considerably easier to complete when your mind is prepared for what it's about to go through. You don't go through that initial shock and indignation of having most of your rights taken away. You also understand that it isn't anything personal, they treat everyone like that; it is part of the process.

Needless to say, drug programs were a way out, but not an easy one and not a very successful one. That didn't leave many other ways out. You either got injured, got sick or died. Not any choices you would choose for yourself, but you are not the one to choose most of the time.

I heard the stories almost every day. I would go visit people in the hospital so often, I knew all the nurses by sight. I went to many funerals, wakes or just gatherings for people who had died. Those could be especially tough because the person's family was sometimes there. They hadn't seen their kid in some time and knew that their child died in a drug lost life. They looked at me very accusingly and I was at a loss for words. What could I possibly say? I wasn't the direct cause of their child's death but I sure didn't do anything to stop it. I always felt guilty around them, like I had done something terribly wrong.

I don't really know why I even go to funerals anymore; I've been to so many and none have been a good experience.

They say that the funeral is the last chance to say "goodbye," but I don't believe that. I never truly said goodbye to any of them. Every time I think of each of them, they are alive again, even just for a short moment. I remember little bits, things that only they and I would remember and I will never say goodbye. The funny thing about it is when I think of them, it's never their funerals. Funerals are the last thing I want to remember about them. I remember moments when I smiled or learned a life lesson from them. You learn life lessons from every single person if you look hard enough and spend enough time with him.

The worst part is the fact that most of them died terrible deaths, in ways you couldn't possibly imagine happening to you.

One guy was thrown off a building for stealing drugs from someone else. Rumor had it Julio had something to do with it but it was never proven.

Julio was a prime example of a 'crankster-gangster.' Usually if they had a gangster reputation, I steered clear. They were always way more trouble than they were worth, and they always expected special treatment because they were gangsters and everyone was supposed to give them deals.

I knew a prostitute who was beaten and killed by a 'John' and left by one of the piers. Another guy was stabbed to death when he was supposed to be dealing with friends. A couple different people were shot over a bad drug deal or something even more ridiculous, over a verbal argument.

A Mini bus hit one guy I guess he thought he could outrun it. They even found a guy I knew all cut up in a box back in an alley behind Polk Street.

Polk Street was a main shopping avenue for male prostitutes in San Francisco. That was never my chosen profession, but the guys up there bought a lot of dope. They were just really flaky to deal with, so I didn't go up there very often. The civic center was my stomping grounds.

That was only a small portion of the total. Most of the deaths were from overdoses or AIDS. AIDS is a whole different story. You watch them slowly waste away to nothing, just hollow, tired shells of which they use to be. In that condition, they can't fight off any kind of sickness, so something usually insignificant can destroy them. I really hated visiting them in the hospital.

Hospitals were depressing enough with all the sad families sitting around, some crying. Going there to see someone that probably isn't getting out really sucks. They are hooked up on all sorts of machines. An oxygen tube out of their nose makes it hard for them to talk. Pneumonia was the main culprit, causing the lungs to fill with liquid; the person can't get enough oxygen to survive and slowly suffocates. The first time I saw someone like that struggling for breath and heard the bubbling sound coming from inside his chest affected me the most. When breathing is second nature, it's hard to watch someone struggle to take each breath.

Every time I walked up to a hospital bed the person lying there lit up. They would be so thrilled just to have a visitor. It's heart breaking when I think of how many people in there died without a visitor or someone to hold their hand. Many people with this disease died alone with no family or friends around. What a lonely way to go.

Going to the hospital was different for me than going to funerals. At the hospital, sometimes I really did get to say a last goodbye. Holding someone's hand when he needed it the most giving him a chance to say goodbye and just being there with him at the end was all he wanted; who could say no to that?

CHAPTER 10
LIFE AT THE END OF A GUN

At this point in my life, all things were centered around surviving each day with food in my stomach, clothes on my back, and drugs in my system, not necessarily in that order. All the days kind of blurred together and things get a little mixed up. I remember everything that happened, but not necessarily in the correct order. Days became weeks and weeks turned into months as I fell further into this underworld that no one every really sees until he becomes a part of it. At that point, it becomes all you see.

I met a lot of colorful characters on the way, so I thought I'd take a little time to include them; this may be the one and only time they will ever be written about, since most are dead by now and the rest are locked up in prison. Besides the people I've mentioned so far, there were always the people you met who have dropped out of society on purpose or by accident, and have some made up name they go by now. There was Big Bill, Tweaky Tony, Flaco, Sundance, Bicycle Bill, Cat-Man, Slam-a-Gram Sam, and many other names that obviously weren't their names when they were kids. Even my friend, John, had the nickname Mohawk John, due to his unusual choice of hairstyles. I actually earned the nickname Honest Aaron when I was dealing, which I kind of liked. It's not every day that you can call a drug dealer honest. My honesty is what got me up in the higher area of dealing and making money. It also got my name noticed by some people that I wish had never heard my name. As soon as some found out that a seventeen year old kid had a big bag of dope, a lot of money and wasn't some gun-toting gangster, he became fair game for an easy mark. But nothing ever is as easy as it looks.

Some people that I met along the way were pretty scandalous. They would screw over pretty much anyone if they thought that they could get away with it. They only needed to get away with it long enough to get out of your sight. They figured that the odds were on their side whether they might or might not run into you again on the streets. Most of the time they were correct in that assumption. Unfortunately, when their luck ran out, and they always pushed their luck until it just had to run out, it was usually very messy and dramatic. Mark Red Cloud was probably the most scandalous of the lot, well, in his own special way. Every time I ran into him he was either hiding from someone he'd ripped off, plotting some devious scandal that he was about to partake in, or just running around acting like a very animated cartoon character. When he was really high I use to think he reminded me of Sylvester the Cat. He always had a plan that ended with him having everything. I bet he was a really fast runner, with all the practice he got.

You could always tell when he had just got over on somebody. He was high as a kite, jumping around and looking for more dope. This was always a fun time to run into Mark. He had a pocket full of money and a really good story to go with it. But you always had to keep in mind that this was Mark's side of the story. He always had his reason for doing it; sometimes the reason was because they were stupid enough to trust him. He had told me more than one story of him dealing with someone. That person told Mark, "I heard that some guy named Mark Red Cloud was a rip-off and not to deal with him." This was while he was talking them into giving him their money while they waited for him to come back. He really got a kick out of taking their money. He was scandalous all the way down to his name, Mark Red Cloud. He was a thin white guy with reddish-brown hair, maybe Irish. I don't know how many Red Clouds there are in Ireland, but I am sure he doesn't belong to them.

One day Mark Red Cloud came hustling up to me with a pretty girl in tow and a whole wad of cash. He said he just ripped some guy off and stole his girlfriend. She wanted to get high, so that's where I came in. He even offered her to me, but there was no way I was about to get mixed-up in some Mark Red Cloud shit. There were always bad repercussions

I sold him some dope and went into Carl's JR's restaurant to get a soda and just sit down. I always sat next to the front windows so I could watch what was going on out in the Civic Center. I could see who was walking around, if there was anyone I knew, and if there were any cops out there. Not ten minutes later Mark Red Cloud went flying through the plaza with some big guy with a baseball bat chasing behind him, closing the gap. The girl was nowhere to be seen, probably running the opposite direction.

I never did find out if it was the girl's boyfriend who was chasing him or someone else he burned in the past. To him, I guess it really didn't matter. Fear is fear and you run, no matter who it is, just another day in the life of Mark Red Cloud.

One day I got a phone call from one of the many people who called for drugs. He said he had 400 dollars to spend and wanted to know if I could help him out. I said yeah, and that I would meet him a few blocks down from my house. I put a bunch of dope in my jacket (one of the intricate arts of being a tweaker is finding all of the unique places on your person that you can hide your drugs), and headed down to the corner where I was supposed to meet him. He was standing on the corner, looking about as suspicious as possible, obviously still high from the last bag of meth he had done earlier that day. When he saw me, he walked over and said hi.
He said he had the money in his truck and we should walk down to it to

complete the deal, out of sight from the public. Of course I was all for that, the less conspicuous the better. We got down to the truck and when I opened the passenger side door, there was an infamous gangster in there who I knew from passing by. His name was Julio, and everyone had warned me to stay as far away from him as possible. So any time anyone said they were getting dope for Julio, I always told them I was out, feeling that safe is much better than sorry in that situation. I never figured that the fact of avoiding him was just adding fuel to his uncontrolled fire, and that we would meet eventually. Well, Julio had a gun in his hand and said, "Get in!" Hard to argue with that. I got in the passenger side and he started ranting about how I've disrespected him and this is what happens to people that disrespect him, blah blah blah. Respect was always a large issue in everyone I met along this road. To bad none of them realized it at the time, it's impossible to have any respect for someone who would rob friend or foe for a hit and do anything they can to make a little cash.

Julio said, "OK, time to pay up. What you got on you?"

I lied to him and said I only had a 1/16th of an ounce on me (worth 120 bucks) and 30 dollars. I kept all my money and drugs in separate places, just in case this might happen. So I pulled out that, and he checked those pockets to make sure that was everything, and told me to get the fuck out of the truck. When I got out, I was shaking, I don't think from the robbery or the gun, but from anger. I was furious, and all I could think about was how to get back at this guy. I walked back down the streets to my house, running the whole thing over in my head, with my left hand in a pocket that he didn't check, rubbing about a thousand dollars in cash that he never even knew I had on me. When I got back to my apartment, it was full of tweakers, which was normal, and I walked in and slammed the door shut. Everyone got real quiet, I guess because it was my house, and if they didn't at least fake interest in my problems, they might be out the door and no more dope.

I told everyone that I had just got robbed, and as I went over the story again, and remembered how the gun shook in Julio's hand, I just got angrier that this had happened to me. I knew that the tweaker world I lived in was very small and close and that whatever I said would get back to him, maybe a little twisted around by then, but he would hear something. So, I planned what I would say carefully, thinking about it the whole walk back to my house. I wasn't sure how I would get even, but as far as I was concerned, he had something coming from me. I knew he had a big ego, and he would let whatever he heard I said work him up into a frenzy. By the time I got to the apartment, I had it pretty well thought out, and I was seriously going to hurt this guy.
I kept telling myself that he could have shot me, that he pulled a gun on me, and that he stole from me.

So, after coming in and slamming the door, everyone got quiet and asked what had happened. I wasn't even sure that one of these people didn't have something to do with it, so I was careful about what I said.

I said, "That punk Julio just pulled a gun on me! He tried to rob me!" Everyone asked if he got anything and what had happened. I took off my jacket, and as I told the story about how he got a 1/16th and 30 dollars from me, the whole while I proceeded to pull out 15 more 1/16ths and over a thousand dollars out of the jacket. I said, "That little bitch can't even pull a robbery right, he didn't get hardly any of this stuff, and now he's made an enemy for life." Everyone thought it was very humorous that Julio got away with so little and I came back with almost everything. I even pointed out that they had set me up by requesting four hundred dollars worth of dope, but didn't even think to question why I didn't have even that much on me at the time. I knew this was going to get back to him, and it would just start a small war between him and me, but I had my motives for it. I wasn't even close to calling this even or over. But I needed to make this situation a little more even.

I called my friend, David, who was always first in helping me find ways to get myself into trouble, and asked him where I could get a gun.

He laughed and said, "It's about time you thought about protecting yourself. All the assholes in this world have one, you need to make it even."

I told him about what had happened with Julio and how I was going to get even. I told him about my whole plan, and what I needed. I told him that all I needed from him was a gun and for him to spread it around that whoever tells me where I can find Julio will get a gram of meth. Amazing what people will do for a bag of dope. I would like to think that the reason people gave up where Julio was at was that they felt bad about what happened to me, but I know they only did it for the drugs. I know that now and figured that then, but it was a nice hope that some people cared about fairness and justice.

David suggested that I talk to this girl we knew, Stacia. She had a friend who inherited four million dollars and spent it all on mail order catalogs over a three-year period. So even though he was broke now, he had a house full of stuff, most of it still in boxes unopened. So I called Stacia and told her about what had happened. She felt sort of guilty in an offhand way because she was Julio's friend, and if she had known what was going to happen, she didn't do anything to stop it or warn me.
She said she would go over to her friend's house and see what he had there. The next day she called and said for me to stop by, she had something she wanted to

show me. When I got there she was pretty high. Whether it was due to dope or the thrill of the situation she was helping to create, I wasn't so sure about.

She said, "Look at what I got", and pulled out a stun gun, like the kind you can buy for self protection that sends a burst of electricity through someone and is supposed to stop him dead in his tracks. But not really what I was looking for. She was way too excited over the stun gun, but I didn't want to burst her bubble, so I thanked her and told her this was perfect. I asked her if she wanted anything for it, cash or anything. But she replied that she just got it for me because I asked. Well, I wasn't just going to take it from her for free, so I gave her a gram. Her eyes lit up when she saw the dope, and even though she didn't want anything for it, she was still happy to get some dope. I picked up the stun gun and started to leave. I turned towards the door and as I took a step, she said, "If that doesn't do it for you, maybe this will." When I turned around she was holding a brand new nine-millimeter SIG.-SAR pistol in her hand. She was waving it around like a toy, and in her excitement (she was a little strange), she put the pistol in her mouth and pulled the trigger. I heard a very loud click and my heart was thumping loud enough to hear it. But there was just a click. She spun the gun around her finger with the trigger guard, laughing, and said it wasn't loaded. I was shocked that she actually got me a gun. I asked her what she wanted for it. She said nothing; she said it was from a three-gun collection her friend had and he didn't even know it was missing. It was kept in a box and only had been used on a firing range.

She looked at me all serious and said, "I know what you are gonna do with this, and I've got a plan. If you use it and give it back to me, I can put it back in my friend's gun collection, where it will never be seen again, and he'll never be the wiser." It kind of scared me how she seemed to have planned a little of this out herself, and that she was talking about Julio, with whom she was supposed to be friends. I guess living this lifestyle, everyone develops a little gangster attitude eventually. But I agreed that it was a good plan, mostly to just get the gun. I had no idea what, if anything, I was going to do with the gun or what would happen to it later on down the road.

Now all I had to do was wait until some tweaker turned in Julio's whereabouts for the bag of dope. That didn't take long; maybe even the next day someone called me and said the knew Julio was up in a hotel room in the same hotel Stacia lived in, one floor above her, visiting someone. Jokingly, the person said, they are probably getting high on the dope he stole from you.
I told the person that it might be the last hit he ever enjoys, and that quieted the person's jovial mood; he asked what I was going to do. I told him never mind all that, and I would meet him in Stacia's room to pay him for the info.

I called Stacia and told her what was happening. She thought it was very amusing that it was all going to play out in her own hotel, and even offered to go up there and shoot him herself. I told her to stay out of it, that this was my problem to deal with how I saw fit. I headed to the hotel, running over and over in my head what happened in that truck and building up this fury inside of me. I kept telling myself that he had this coming, and if not from me, then from someone else he ripped off in the past. But I knew that if I settled this, took action, it would be like the bully problem I went through. I would set an example and things would lighten up for me.

I called Stacia again from the lobby of the hotel and she came down to let me in. You could tell she was really into this and was getting quite a thrill from it. She snuck me up the back staircase to her room so no one would see me enter. We didn't say a word until we were in her room alone with the guy who originally called me. He was still hanging out waiting for payment. Stacia said that while I was on my way over he came to her room and said that I told him to wait there for me. She asked him what he had told me, and when she found out what room Julio was in, she went up there to check. She knew the guy Julio was visiting, so she went up there and asked if he had a needle she could borrow or have. Needles were a dime a dozen, and there were a lot of places you could go to get new ones, but no one ever wanted to go because of the fear that undercover cops were watching the needle exchange places to see who was using. So, instead, everyone just shared and borrowed needles. I even saw a group of people who had one needle between them (and the needle was dull) so before they took turns using it, one person sharpened it with the striker on the back of a matchbook. Now, that's gotta be good for you.

She told me that when she went up there, Julio was still there and he didn't look like he was leaving any time soon. I hadspent the past half hour getting myself angry enough to do something stupid and regrettable, but I felt he had it coming and that he could have just as easily shot me. I had heard other people talking about guns and such, and I remember how a few of them made the same statement "If they pull a gun on me they better plan to use it because if they don't, they had better be looking over their shoulder for the rest of their life.

I went up to the next floor, almost directly above Stacia's room. I told Stacia to stay down in her room, to keep someplace open if I needed to come back down, but I had no intention of returning to her room. I was heading out of the hotel, no matter what happened.
When I got near the door, I could hear two people talking in the room, and I knew the other person in there, but I also knew he would leave if I asked him to; he had no ties with Julio, just the fact that they were getting high together at the moment. So I took a deep breath and kicked the door open. Julio was in the

process of hitting himself with his needle, and his eyes grew as wide as saucers when he saw me at the door. When he looked down and saw the gun, they grew even more wide and he knew he was about to have a life changing experience. He turned to the window, with the syringe still in his arm, and jumped out. Two stories down he hit the pavement and from what I understand, he broke his leg. All I know is he left a 1/4 ounce (four times as much as he took from me) of meth sitting on the table and ran. I looked out the window, mainly because I was curious how far down it was, I had no idea.

When I looked out, Stacia was leaning out of her window, one floor down, and said she heard and saw everything. She said, "He jumped out, landed kind of funny on one leg, and ran down the alley limping badly. Are you gonna go after him?" I think she just wanted to see someone get hurt; she seemed to have that little streak buried deep down inside of her. I told her to get her head back in her room, and that I'd be down there in a second. Then I pulled my head back in the room to look at Michael, the guy whose room it was. He was shocked silent. It was kinda funny really, Michael couldn't shut up if he had to in any normal situation, but this may have been just too much for his already overloaded system. At this point I was starting to find this whole situation rather funny. I asked Michael, "Whose dope is this sitting on the mirror?"

Michael swallowed and laughed nervously, "Well, it was Julio's, but he seems to have been in a big hurry to leave. So I guess it's yours now. I've never seen Julio take off like that before. He must have really fucked you over, huh?"

I said, " He was the first and last person to ever rob me at gun point. When you see him, please tell him that I took all of his dope, and if he wants it back, he can feel free to come ask me for it."

I picked up the bag of white powder and before leaving, poured some of it back on the mirror and said, "This is for you. Don't tell Julio I gave you any. Just tell him that I took it all and left looking for him." He looked at me astonished and said thanks for the dope. It was free dope anyway, what the hell, he didn't freak out and scream or run out of the room. He just sat there through the whole ordeal and watched it play out. That's one sure thing about tweakers, if they haven't done some outrageous things, they've definitely witnessed some.

I went back down to Stacia's room and told her what happened. I asked her whether she thought I had just started a war with Julio or just ended one.
She said that she had no idea, but she did know that as well as being a prick, Julio was a coward too. So he may just find that there are easier pickings elsewhere.

I've seen Julio since this incident, but the whole situation was different. My girlfriend, at the time when I saw Julio next, seemed to hold a lot of power over the entire group of so-called gangsters that I frequented. He was as nice as humanly possible then, like nothing had ever happened. But then again, my girlfriend at the time got a guy beat up three times, by different people, because he had the poor luck of choosing her car to break into. We will just call her my girlfriend later on down the road, because I'm not so sure she would be happy about me including her name in this. I'm not too concerned about the rest of the people I talk about because I know more than half of them have definitely passed away, and it's easy to assume the other half have as well, by now. We led a hard and rough life and most of us died young.

One thing for sure, the whole incident was talked about many times after this, between a lot of different people in this small circle, sometimes with the facts getting stretched out of proportions. But it was talked about, and it made the next person think before deciding that I might be an easy target.

CHAPTER 11
JON

Jon was a very interesting character. He had his good and his bad, just like the rest of us. I've just never seen karma catch up with a person like it has with Jon. I go to see him once or twice a month at the assisted living house he stays at. It's a very depressing place with many very sad people in it, all seeming to be waiting to die. I think there is a point in each person's life where he finally just gives up living and is tired of the day-to-day routine of life. Especially if he has some sort of debility that can never be overcome. Jon is that way now. The last time I spoke with him, he told me about how he has finally found his last stop in life, the house he lives in now. It's a big step to take in life when you decide that it's almost over and you don't have much time left. Reality can come crashing down around you and it's very easy to get caught up in the emotions and try to go out with a bang. I've had a few friends try that, most with a very bad endings.

Jon was a very close friend who would have done anything for me, but he had his criminal side as well. I think he saw himself as a modern day Robin Hood, steal from the rich, and give to himself, who happened to be poor. Every time I saw him he had some sort of new toy, a new bike, a new car, a new motorcycle... and none of them belonged to him. Meth has a way of making people do things they would never do otherwise, and Jon was no exception. But he was always smiling and laughing and seemed to be having a good time ripping and roaring in this crazy little speed world.

He came riding up to me one day at the Civic Center on a new motorcycle. I said, "Nice bike, where'd you get it?"

Jon smiled devilishly and said, " I borrowed it from a friend," which meant that he stole it and that he would not have it long.

As we were talking with a few other friends, a cop car pulled up on the sidewalk in front of us. They harassed us a lot for loitering around there. I'm sure they knew what we were up to, and probably wouldn't have hassled us so much if we weren't right out in the public, looking like we did then. As soon as one of the officers got out of the patrol car, Jon knew he had to get ghost. He was sitting on the bike already, and it had been running the whole time, so as soon as the cop was about half way, Jon was off like a rocket. He shot up the sidewalk right past a statue, down three steps and he was out on the street. The cop ran back to car and they began pursuing. I read the police report later on and found out what happened after they left our sight, at least the police officer's view of what happened.

My friend David also took off on his mountain bike to see what was going to happen. It was like a scene out of a movie. A few different people had stories about how they managed to outrun the cops on a motorcycle. This just wasn't one of those times.

They raced up and down streets; the report says they pursued him for seventeen blocks. It all came to a sudden end about eight blocks away from where it all started. Jon was flying through intersections, and barely missing cars at each crossing, until he got to Divisadero Street. It's a fairly busy street with a lot of traffic on it. Jon T-boned a car in the intersection and drove his bike straight into the rear driver's side door of a car, pushing it over two lanes of traffic. Jon slid over the top of the car and back down on the asphalt, across to the sidewalk where his head hit the curb. This all happened just as David was riding up on his bicycle. I remember him telling me the story an hour later, he had blood on him and he was really shook up by all the action and gore.

Jon lost about eight inches of his skullcap and was never the same again. Head injuries completely change person, physically, emotionally, and mentally. I think Jon's definition of right and wrong from that point on got a little more tilted. He was never the same again, but after a few surgeries, he had a reconstructed skull and he got right back into the drug scene. After a few years back in the game, his karma truly caught up with him one night. He was robbed and beaten and re-injured his head, but a lot worse this time. Now he will never be the same. He can't walk very well, and has trouble remembering things and concentrating. When I visited him, at times I could see the old Jon, from back in the day, but other times he just seemed very old and tired.

I get this swell of emotions, sorrow, anger, and the feeling that life is totally unfair sometimes. I think how glad I am to be out of it and leading a semi-normal life now. I realize how close I came to being in the same situation that Jon is in, and I wonder if I would even want to still be around when life came crashing down upon me like that. The fact of the matter is that Jon did survive, unlike many others I've run into along the way.

I remember the first day I went to see Jon in the hospital, after not seeing him for four years. He was sitting in the lunch area of the hospital that he resided in. He was playing an electronic poker game they had there for the patients to entertain themselves. Years ago he had lost hundreds of dollars on the same type of machine, but this machine didn't use money. I thought it was a big coincidence that he would be playing the same game, but I never mentioned it.

I stayed back for a moment and just watched. His movements were slow and deliberate and he seemed to have to think about everything he did before he actually tried to do it. After a few moments I decided to walk up and say hi. He looked up blankly, and then I saw recognition in his eyes. He looked really excited, like he didn't get many visitors, which turned out to be true. After a few minutes he asked how my wife was and my little girl. I was surprised that he even knew I had a little girl; I guess that someone else who visited him must have told him about my daughter. I didn't want to get into things too deeply, so rather than telling him about my wife and I being separated, I just said that they were fine and that she said to say hi. Then a nurse came up and told Jon that it was lunchtime. After a few minutes, they brought him a plastic tray with what looked like boiled chicken and little serving of veggies and dessert. I asked him if he was allowed to go out. He said sure, they let him come and go as he pleased. So I asked if he wanted to go out to lunch.

The nurses really cared about Jon and seemed to be thrilled that he had a visitor. They constantly checked on him, and even though he lived there, they tried to allow him as much freedom as possible, scheduling a few outings and not asking him where he was going if he wanted to go out. But it was still a hospital. People died there every day, and the section Jon lived in was more like a hospice, a place where people go to die. One of his roommates was in the final stages of Multiple Sclerosis and his other roommate had emphysema and was on a constant supply of oxygen.

We walked to his room to get a sweater for him, and he walked in very slow methodical steps. You could see he was concentrating on each step and making each foot land in front of the last. When we got to the room I was starting to get pretty optimistic. He seemed OK at first glance. A little motor control problem, but otherwise things didn't seem too bad. As we got to his room, he stopped in the doorway and had this puzzled look on his face. I asked if he forgot something, and he laughed and said he forgot a lot of things. At this point the realization of what had happened to him finally hit home. He looked really embarrassed, and said he had a question for me. I said, sure, shoot, what's the question? After about twenty minutes with him, he looked me in the eyes and said, " For the life of me, I can't remember your name."

Jon and I had known each other for a very long time and it really shook me up when he asked that. I acted like it was no big deal and told him my name was Aaron. That was the point the realization began. Even after telling him my name, I could tell that he hadn't just forgot it, but that it was completely gone from his memory. I just smiled and played it off, but that moment really affected me, realizing that this could have been any one of us, and how lucky I was to still have all my faculties and memories.
We got his sweater and went down to my car. I asked him where he'd like to eat,

anywhere, just name it. He said he hadn't been to Mc Donald's in over three years, so that's where we went. I didn't eat much, just mainly watched Jon destroy a Big Mac. He apologized about the mess but I just laughed and told him that all that was important was that he enjoyed it. He said it was the best meal he'd had in years. After spending the day with Jon, I decided that I was going to spend many more with him in the near future. I took him out walking around the city, to baseball games, and out to eat as often as I could.

I had to throw out my old address book because three out of four people in it had a line drawn through their name. Many people's lives, with untold talents and dreams, ended as quickly as snuffing out the flame on a candle. 'Here one day, gone the next.' I heard that statement often during this whole time. If it wasn't from death, it was from going to jail or prison. People would vanish for three months to a year, and then re-appear, a little fatter, a little healthier, and ready to start the downward spiral into addiction all over again. They spent their time locked up thinking about where they would get their first hit, what hustle they might try to support their habit, and how they could get over on their probation or parole officer. I will get into the whole prison aspect of this story later on; I happen to have a very up close and personal view on that subject.

CHAPTER 12
THE END OF THE DAY

Here is where things begin their sudden and complete change. A friend of mine, Kelly, called me and asked if I was doing anything (which is tweaker code for, do you have any drugs). I said, "Sure, what do you need?"

Kelly said, "Here's my situation." (They always seemed to have situations.) "I am receiving an inheritance of forty thousand dollars and I need a ride up to Yreka to collect it. They will only give it to me if I go there in person. I will give you six hundred dollars to drive me up there and back, plus I want to buy two thousand dollars worth of dope from you."

I saw an easy way to make some fast cash, so I said, "Sure, when and where?"

He said he'd call me back with all the details in an hour. So I hung up the phone and told my girlfriend that Kelly had called and what he wanted. She said, "There is no way you are bringing that dope fiend over to our house. I don't want him and all his tweaker buddies knowing where we live." That was a good point; that was the reason we moved outside the city to begin with. So I packed up a ¼ pound of meth and put it in a backpack in the back of my car. Kelly called an hour later and I told him I would pick him up and take him there, but as soon as we got back to San Francisco we would have to take care of the other business quickly and that I had to head back out of the city. He said sure, no problem with that.

I picked Kelly up on the corner of 7th & Market Street in San Francisco. He was standing there looking completely spun out, digging through his pockets, looking around a lot, and couldn't stand still, kept pacing little circles. I pulled the car up to the curb and yelled out the window, "Get in!"

It was about eight or nine in the morning as we headed across the Golden Gate Bridge northbound towards Marin. As we got to the other end of the bridge, Kelly asked if I had anything he could do? I said sure, but we needed to stop somewhere. At the other end of the bridge is a public park/lookout point that tourists go to when visiting the Golden Gate. We pulled into the parking lot and parked near the restrooms. Kelly got out and went into the bathroom for water for his syringe after I gave him a pretty big hit to do. After sitting in the car for what seemed hours, but was more like twenty minutes, I went into the bathroom to rescue him. Just as I had suspected, he was so spun out, he was washing his hair in the sink, and cleaning the restroom all at once. I told him that we had to go and for him to come on.

We pulled out of the parking lot and headed north again through Marin. I got behind a line of cars in the fast lane and we were all doing about 60 in a 55 zone, when a California Highway Patrol officer pulled up on all of us and pulled all five cars over at once. One by one he went down the row of cars issuing tickets and then releasing each of the law breakers. Of course we were the last of the pack, so all we could do was sit and wait for our turn. The whole while, I was going over in my head what I was going to say to him. I knew that we hadn't really done anything wrong and he was just going to write me a ticket and be on his way, as long as I played it cool. As long as I didn't send up any red flags of suspicion, we should be fine.

He walked up to the window and asked me, " Do you know what I pulled you over for?"

I tried to control my breathing and answered him slowly, "Yes, sir. I was over the speed limit by five miles an hour."

The officer scanned the interior of my car as he said, "Every one of you states that you were only doing five miles over the speed limit, like that makes it OK or something. Exceeding the speed limit is illegal, no matter by how much."

I agreed with him and said that it wouldn't happen again, that we were just passing through Marin on our way up to Yreka. The last thing I wanted to do was piss this guy off. I just wanted my ticket so I could be on my way.

He asked me for my license, registration, and proof of insurance. I already had all the proper papers ready and handed them over to the him. Right before he went back to his car to sit down and write the ticket, he looked over at Kelly and said, "What about you? Do you have a license or California ID?"

Kelly patted his pockets and said, "Sorry officer, I don't have my license on me, but I know my license number."

The officer said ok, pulled out a notepad and wrote down the number Kelly gave him before he walked back to the car. As soon as the cop got out of ear shot, Kelly said, " I hope it doesn't come back that I'm on parole."

I said, "As long as you have been reporting, and you don't have any warrants, you should be fine. Do you have any wants or warrants?"

Kelly laughed nervously and said, "Hehe, not yet I don't, but if I don't go see my parole officer this week, I will." I told him, "Then we should be fine, just don't do anything stupid, OK?" Boy, I would live to regret those words.

I looked back up in the rear view mirror and saw the cop heading back to my window. As he approached, he had a black leather binder in his hand. He got to my car and said, "OK, sign the ticket at the bottom, it's not an admission of guilt, just a promise that you will appear in court."

As he was handing me his ticket book for my signature, he looked over at Kelly and said, "I ran your license number, but I couldn't find you, are you sure that was your correct number?"

Kelly patted his pockets again nervously and then blurted out, "Oh wait a minute, I have a form of ID." Then he pulled out his San Quentin privilege card, (used to move around San Quentin when you are an inmate there), and handed it to the officer. I watched the cops eyes grow wider as he said, "What the... OK, both you kindly get out of the car." At this point I knew the walls were crashing down around me. My heart was in my throat and I could feel it beating so hard that it made it difficult to swallow. He had us come around to the side of the car away from traffic and sit on the ground while he waved for his partner to come out. She walked over and asked what's up?

He laughed and said, "Look what this clown just handed me." He showed the card to the other officer and she didn't smile at all. Now they had all sorts of questions for us: where were we going, why were we going there, why did I have a pager, why did I have a cell phone. They searched both of our pockets and wanted to know why I had seven hundred dollars on me and where did I work to earn that much cash? Then they asked if they could search the car. I said, "No, you can't search the car, and can I have my ticket so we can go? We aren't doing anything wrong here."

The male officer looked over at the female officer and said, "Isn't there a search and seizure law that allows us to search any automobile that a felon on parole is in?" the female officer said, "Yes, and that's what we are going to do."

So while the male cop started to open the passenger-side car door, the other cop handcuffed each of us with our hands behind our back. When he got to the back seat and pulled out the backpack and threw it on the hood of my car, I knew we were dead. He began emptying the pack out on the hood of the car, and when he came across the dope, he called his partner over. Next thing you knew, two more patrol cars pulled up behind the first one and officers walked up to join the search. Unlike Julio, they found the whole stash, and I doubted they were going to give it back. They led both of us to separate cars and we went to the station. At this point I was still too shocked to be pissed at Kelly for what he did.
Later on, when things settled down, I grew angry at the fact that Kelly's prison card was the reason I was in jail. I didn't stop to think that it was the dope in my

backpack, not Kelly's card that did me in.

They took me to a small room in the basement of the station. It was a very plain room with two chairs, a desk, and a phone. They sat me down with my hands still cuffed and asked if I wanted a cigarette. I said yes, and they uncuffed me and let me smoke one. About half way through the smoke they said, "Now here's the deal. Either you are going to be doing a long time in jail, or you are going to help us out here. All we want you to do is make a phone call. Call up your connection and set up a drop somewhere. Then you can go back to life as though this day never happened. One phone call and you are free, we want where you get it from, not you."

I just smirked a little and said, "OK, I get my dope from people who have a lot of friends, in and out of jail. If I don't tell you anything, I do my time and eventually go home. If I set someone up, someone will kill me, no doubt about that. So you tell me, which offer would sound more appealing to you if you were in my shoes?"

The officer turned a bright shade of red and yelled, "Get his fuckin' ass upstairs and book him. And put out that God damned cigarette. You make me fuckin' sick!"

So upstairs I went. They fingerprinted me, took all my clothes and stored them away, gave me a bedroll, and sent me to a cell that held five other prisoners. Now, don't think it happened just like that; it took about eight hours for them to process me in. They take their sweet time doing it, while you sit in a large holding tank with a bunch of other guys that had had a very bad day as well. With my previous stays locked up, I knew a few basic rules.

1. Don't talk to anyone; no one wants to hear anyone else's problems or griefs. They have enough of their own right now.
2. Don't take any shit from anyone. If someone says move, you are in my seat, you tell him to fuck off and look away. They will always test you, to see what you are made of, and I learned early that a lot of it is just mind games they play.
3. If they keep pushing you and won't let up, be the first to strike. Hit them with everything you have and hope that in the end they will have developed enough respect for you to leave you alone in the future. It's easy to find someone in there who won't fight back, so they head towards him.
4. NEVER, under any circumstances, tell! No matter what, it is you against the cops in there. Even though the blacks hated the whites and the blacks

hated other blacks, and Mexicans hated other types of Hispanics, with their north and south gangs, we were still united against the MAN. Never give up another inmate, or there will be hell to pay.
5. Stick to your own kind. It's very segregated in there and that's the way the cops want it. We have separate weight areas, eat at different tables, and never mingle.

So now a whole new life began. Things were different, now and forever. As soon as I got back into the cell that was going to be my home for the next few months, I made a decision that this was it. No more of this crazy lifestyle for me. If and when I ever got out of there, I was going to try to make something out of what life I had left. The fourth day I was there, a nurse came around and was giving each of us a little pinprick to test us for tuberculosis. While she was there, I started talking to her. She was very nice and seemed to actually care about us, which was unusual in there. I told her that I was a speed addict and I planned to change my life. She just kind of smiled and had that look of, yeah, right, like I haven't heard that one before a hundred times. But, I suggested that maybe I should take a test to see if I had anything, and asked if that was possible. She said sure, but not until tomorrow. I knew what the results were gonna be, but I needed to have it done.

The next day, I went to the nurse and gave her some blood. She said that in a week we'd have the results but not to worry. A week later the nurse personally came to my cell, and I knew I was in trouble. She said that I had tested positive for the HIV virus and that I probably had less than a year to live. She tried to tell me about the virus, but I didn't want to listen. I already knew way too much about it, and a few of my friends had already passed away from it.

A few days later a Public Defender came to see me. He asked me if I knew who my judge was going to be. I said that I had no idea. He told me that my judge was confined to a wheelchair, that he was very strict, that there was really nothing he could do for me, and that the district attorney had offered me seventeen years. He suggested that I take the deal because this judge wasn't going to go easy on me, that he had issues with drug addicts. I was shocked. I told him to come back tomorrow and I would have a decision then.

I went back to my cell and called my girlfriend, she was my only source of sanity, if you can call it that. She was losing her mind as well, at home, all alone now, deserted by her other half. But she did have a few suggestions to help me, and I'll never forget her for what she did the first year I was in.
She said that the Public Defender, (I think she called him a public pretender though), was full of shit and that we needed to get a real attorney. So she found me a good attorney who was willing to take my case. I called the Public

Defender and told him he was fired, that I had found private counsel. He told me that I was wasting my money and that the judge wasn't going to budge from the seventeen years. I thanked him for his input and said that I had to find that out on my own, but thank you and goodbye.

A few days before my next court date, my attorney came to see me and discuss the case. He was a very nice, little old man who seemed a little out of his league. I asked him if he knew of the judge I was supposed to be going in front of. He had a very interesting story about the judge. Back in the 1970's, he was the District Attorney involved in a case that had to do with the Black Panthers. During the course of the trial, friends of the defendant attempted a jailbreak from the courtroom. In the end, a lot of people were killed and the District Attorney was shot in the back by the Sheriff's Department and paralyzed from the waist down. After all of that, he was given a seat on the bench, and he's been a terror ever since, like he was taking out all of his anger and hatred for that day on each inmate that came in contact with him. I asked the attorney if there was anything I could do about it, and he said we could ask for a change of venue and get another judge. I told him to try and that I'd see him in court.

Time in jail seems to go by in slow motion. Just as fast as life can fly by outside of the prison system, it goes by twice as slowly inside. If it weren't for books, I might have gone completely insane in there. I read a book every three days or so and there never seemed to be enough books for prisoners, no matter where I went. You sleep a lot when you are in there, as well. You can't always sleep the whole night through, usually because someone is screaming or making noise, guards walking up and down the halls with huge sets of metal keys jingling, or even a group of guys singing. There were four black guys down the hall that were actually pretty good. I much preferred listening to them sing rather than listening to some nutter screaming because he was seeing ghosts or kicking heroin. It is amazing the amount of raw talent that is wasting away in our prison systems. Artists, writers, singers, body builders, athletes, everywhere you look, and many of them with no hope of ever seeing the outside again. Those that did have a parole date seemed to be destined to return to their old ways and return to jail not too long after their release. Some of the artists I met in there were extremely talented. I guess when you have all that spare time to practice, you can become quite good at whatever it is you are doing.

On the day of my next hearing, they woke us up and called out a bunch of names to report to the courthouse. I stepped out of my cell and was immediately handcuffed to a sixty-plus year old man.
He had a little shuffle step when he walked, so our walk to the courthouse took longer than I had planned. I was very curious why this little old man was handcuffed and heading to court with me. He looked like he couldn't hurt a fly.

As well as walking very slowly, he also shook. I could feel his trembling through the handcuffs and on the way there I started up a conversation with him. Trying to alleviate his fears would also help me to not constantly worry about what was going to happen to me.

I said, " Hey, Pops, it's gonna be OK, this is just a short stop in a long life that we all have to go through. What in the hell did you do to be handcuffed to me and on your way to court?"

His voice was very shaky but he answered me slowly and sounded terrified while he talked. He said, "I was arrested for drunk driving. I've never been in trouble with the law before and I'm scared that I'm in a lot of trouble."

Drunk driving is a stupid thing to do, but nothing to be terrified about. I told him what I knew about it, hoping it would calm him down a bit. I sure didn't want to see him have a heart attack or stroke.

I said, "Well, you will probably have to pay out the nose for this. I've heard that a drunk driving conviction can cost about ten grand when all is said and done, fines, court costs, drunk driving school, increased insurance costs, and other miscellaneous costs. But besides that, you should be OK. This is your first time in trouble, they will look at that and give you a break." Boy, was I ever wrong. This is when I got my first experience of the wheelchair judge.

They locked us up in a holding tank right outside the courtroom where we sat for hours. They would call us out in groups of two, each group handcuffed and escorted in and out of the courtroom by two guards. We weren't allowed to bring anything with us to court, so there was no reading or writing, just sitting and thinking. I had way too much time to just sit and think in there, running over and over in my head that this might be my last stop in life. I didn't want to die in prison, but after finding out I was positive, it had become a very grim possibility. The nurse didn't try to sugar coat it; she told me that I would die, she just couldn't tell me when, a true reality check when you are still a teenager. But that was at the bottom of my list of issues right then. I would worry about all that after I found out what was going to happen to me.

When it was our turn to go in, they called us out and my new friend started trembling again. We shuffled into the courtroom and it was very quiet. I saw my attorney standing off to the side waiting for me to get in. As I walked up to the table they wanted us to sit at, he stood up and patted me on the shoulder.
He whispered that he would talk to me after the hearing. At this point, they had both of us sit down, which was a good thing, because I was afraid that the old man was close to passing out. They called the old man's name first so he stood

up.

The judge didn't look so bad; actually he looked kind of small and frail. The judge read out the charges and then asked the old man what his plea was. The old man said that he was very sorry and he was pleading guilty. The judge smiled and said something about making an example (I came to see that he said that often) and sentenced the old man to sixteen months in prison. The old man just broke down. He started crying right there in the courtroom. As if the judge didn't even see what happened, he went right on to read my name off. He asked me how I pled, but before I could say a word, I felt that hand on my shoulder and my attorney spoke up for me. He said that my plea was not guilty and we would like to set a date for the next hearing. They said some other things too, but I couldn't concentrate on what they were talking about. All I could hear was this little old man sobbing and hitching his breath. We were escorted back to the holding tank and then escorted back to our cells at the jail.

About an hour later, my attorney had me brought to a private visiting room so we could talk. He told me that he asked for a change of venue, but that every person in front of this judge was asking for one, so I wasn't going to get one. So I was stuck with this guy, good or bad. Unfortunately, I had yet to see any good, just all bad. I told him about my test results and how I wanted to get into a drug program. I had never tried to clean up before. After finding out you have AIDS, you really stop to reconsider everything and where your life is headed. As I said before, I didn't want to die in prison. Now, that fear was becoming more of a reality. He said that a program was a good idea, and I needed to bring this idea up to the judge. He didn't want the judge to think it was my attorney's idea, he wanted the judge to know that it was mine alone. After our meeting, I didn't see him again until my next court date.

Like before, we were escorted up to the courthouse in a group again. This time there was no little old man, though. I figured he was on his way to San Quentin or already there. We sat quietly in the holding tank. I'm sure we each had a lot going through our heads, but it was personal stuff that no one wanted to share with people they didn't even know, especially with a group of prisoners. I just went over in my head what I was going to say to the judge.

Eventually, I was called in and took my place at the table again. When it was my turn to speak, I started slowly and deliberately, choosing my words carefully. I tried to put out of my mind the last time I was here and what happened to the old man. For me, it would be different.
I told the judge about my drug addiction and about testing positive. I told him that I had never tried a program before, but I was willing to give it everything I had because cleaning up was what I wanted. I told him that I felt I had

extenuating circumstances and that prison wouldn't be of any benefit for me, while a program would. I explained how I needed help to stop this endless cycle of addiction and a program would offer that help. I showed him that I had looked around for different programs and had been accepted into two different ones. Then, I changed my plea from not guilty to guilty and threw myself on the mercy of the court. After that, I felt totally drained and just wanted this to all be over.

The judge was quiet for a second before responding. He told me, "You are a menace to society. You will never amount to anything and the only thing I can do for the safety of the community is sentence you to seven years in prison."

And that was it, case closed. They escorted me out of the room and back to my cell eventually, so I had a chance to call and talk to my girlfriend and get her opinion on the whole situation. When I called her, she just cried and cried. I think she kept it together pretty well during all this so far, but now she was as lost as I was. All alone out there, we had kept each other together, through the good and the bad. We complimented each other's personalities.

One day, before it was time for me to ship out to the big house, she came to visit me. She had a puppy with her that she sat up on the visiting room ledge in front of the window. It was the cutest little thing, and you could tell that it loved her. She told me that it rode with her to visit me, riding in the passenger seat so she could use the carpool lane. I thought that was hilarious. The fact that she was able to make me laugh, even in times like this, made me remember why I was with her. She was the day to my night.

A few days later, at eight A.M. they came around and called a few names. My name was on the list, so I knew what time it was. The only things I took with me were the letters from my girlfriend; I left everything else behind. I must have read those letters twenty times already, and I would read them a hundred times more in the next few months. Reading and writing was my only true link with sanity at this point. I was off on a new adventure, a dangerous one, with no idea what was going to happen or how it might turn out. The only benefit I think I had at the time was the fact that a few of my friends from back in the day were already in prison, which prison I had no idea. But, I figured, I would see someone I knew eventually. I really just didn't want to be all alone. The same little voice that pushed me into writing this book may have driven me crazy if I was completely alone in there with no one to talk to. So, off I went to a place I would prefer to never go back to, but if I ever did, at least now I knew how to survive there.
I would be entering a situation with a whole different outlook this time. I guess that's the outlook all my friends developed when they continually returned for

one parole violation or another.

CHAPTER 13
EYES WIDE OPEN

The bus ride was very short; as soon as we got on the bus, we seemed to be getting off. No one really said anything to anyone else. It didn't feel much different than waiting in the holding tank for court. Some of us were on our way there for the very first time, and spent the ride trying to prepare ourselves for what we might be in store for. The rest were on that revolving door called parole and heading back to San Quentin is almost like heading home. I could tell which ones had been there before as soon as we arrived. They would walk around staring in one direction, unlike the rest of us, who would look all around and try to take in what we were seeing. Concrete and iron everywhere. It smelled of sweat, concrete and iron. Everything echoed as well. You could hear your footsteps echo everywhere you went, as well as the jingling of the guards' keys, which I had become accustomed to by now.

They headed us off the bus and into waiting cages, so we could go through the long process of intake. We first were shown all of the belongings that we had stored at the county jail, and were told that we could send the stuff home if we had money on our books to do so; otherwise it would be disposed of. Later on, I found out that disposed of didn't necessarily mean thrown away, it could also mean taken by a prison guard or inmate that worked in R and R (reception and release). There was a lot of nice jewelry that disappeared that way. Fortunately, I was able enough to send my belongings to my girlfriend, rather than having them disposed of. I could hear a few different arguments going on around me between the inmates and prison guards about their belongings. I really didn't blame the inmates, but I don't think I would have said much if they decided to trash all of my things. I would have kept my mouth shut and, as we liked to say, "tried to stay off the officer's radar."

After an hour in there waiting for everyone else to get their things boxed up and set to be mailed out to someone on the outside, we were herded to another cage farther in. One at a time, we were fingerprinted, vital stats were taken, and we were photographed. It was that picture you always seem to see, with a hardened looking person and a board under their chin with one letter and five numbers. No one ever smiled for that picture, but I did manage a small smirk. That number was what we went by from this point on. Even though it's been many years since this, I still remember and will probably never forget my prison number, E-50530. All of my mail came to that number. If I needed to get anywhere throughout the institution, my prison ID, with that picture and my prison number were required. You had to use this card for canteen once a month, to buy essentials like coffee, cigarettes, shower items, and some zu-zus and wham-whams (food and sweets).

When you went to work, you had to show the guards the ID to get from one place to another. You needed this ID to go to the visiting room, see a doctor, go to church or go up to the school. The irony that it was this exact ID that was the reason I was here in the first place didn't get by me. Every day, when I looked at that ID, I was reminded that a little piece of laminated paper could hold so much power. After I got out, my girlfriend kept that card and even told me that it was one of the best pictures there was of me. I didn't have the heart to tell her what that card truly meant to me. I just let her keep it, and tried not to show the goose bumps I got every time she pulled it out of her purse.

This long process took a couple of hours, so all we could do was sit and wait. We were given these bright orange jump suits to wear, and a bundle containing, underclothes, soap, a towel, toothbrush, roll of toilet paper, and a scratchy wool blanket.

I rolled my blanket up into a tight roll, and used it as a pillow. I laid down on the cold concrete and stared up at the ceiling waiting for the whole intake to be done and over with.

When every person was finished being photographed, we were taken to our new home, a concrete rectangle 4ft by 10 ft. We were escorted out of Receiving & Release and over to West Block. On the way a few of the guys were recognized by some of the inmates on the yard. I heard a couple different names being called out, waiting to see if anyone recognized me. Right now, I felt completely alone and just hoped that I would see someone I knew soon. Nobody out in yard called my name, but it wouldn't be long before I found a few of the old crew.

West Block looked like a huge cement warehouse with iron doors to enter it. Once you walked in there, you knew that you weren't in Kansas anymore. Inside the building were five stories of cells, all back to back. There was a wide staircase at both ends of the block, which zigzagged up from floor to floor. It was as if they had built a building inside another building. There was the block that contained all of the prisoners' cells, and around the outside wall at about twenty feet up was a catwalk with a prison guard walking on it carrying a rifle. Twenty feet above him was another catwalk with another armed guard. At each of the four corners of both catwalks was a red painted metal garbage can. On the walk-in I noticed at least four large white signs with bold black print that clearly stated, "No warning shots fired." That and the rifled guards sent chills down my spine.

While we were in Receiving & Release, we were each give three numbers, the first number told us what floor in West Block we were headed to, and the last two numbers told us what cell.

My number was 331, so I only had to walk halfway up those wide stairs and then all the way down to my cell. There was a lot of yelling going on, most of it by people who were just so lonely they wanted to hear the sound of their own voice. There were four cages on the bottom floor, only wide and deep enough for one guy to stand in. Three of the cages were full at the time of our arrival. Before heading up the stairs, the two guards at the head of our group stopped by the cages and explained that any trouble from us would result in our detention in one of these black-screened cages we now stood in front of.

Like teasing monkeys at the zoo, the guard who was speaking yelled, "Isn't that right fellas?" and hit one of the cages as hard as he could with his baton. Instantly, the prisoner in the cage answered in agreement and also asked if he could get out now. The guard told him to shut the fuck up. That caused a little bit of irritation with the other inmates who were in their cells, but close enough to hear what was going on. Suddenly, about thirty or forty guys started yelling at the offensive guard. He just smiled and ignored the uproar. You could tell from the very beginning that he was one of those types that got off on his job. Maybe they were picked on as kids, like me, and found this a perfect way to get back at their tormentors. Or maybe they were just like the bullies I ran across as a child who never grew out of that evil desire to watch others endure misery, as well as helping that misery along if they could. Guards with that type of attitude made up about seventy-five percent. The other twenty-five percent were men who were just there to collect a paycheck or guys who really seemed to give a small bit of sympathy and pity to the inmates and realized that they weren't that different from the men they presided over. The majority of the turnkeys in here (because that's about all they do) were assholes. They enjoyed seeing if they could push a guy to the point of making some really bad decision. They expected you to kiss their asses, and if you didn't, they would make an example out of you. I was that example quite often, but it wasn't really that bad because I never kissed an ass. And since I understood where these cops were coming from and why they were the way they were, it made it easy to accept their harassment and just move on. Most of the time I just smiled and nodded, not really hearing anything they were saying, just waiting for them to finish their yelling so I could go back to my cell to be by myself. Well, as alone as I would ever be in there.

I walked down the hallway to my cell, listening to yelling going on all around me. A lot of noise about new fish and fresh meat; it was pretty obvious it was about us new guys. When I got to my cell it was already open and there was someone in it. I said hi, and he said hi back. He was about five inches shorter than me and looked about fifty years old. Compared to my age, he was ancient. He looked like weathered old biker, which was exactly what he was. He had a scar or birthmark that came up out of the top of his jumpsuit, along his neck and up the side of his face almost to his ear.

But he was intelligent and since all we had to do in there was sit and talk, it was nice to be with someone who could hold a conversation. Fortunately, he had a lot to say, and I had a lot to learn. He told me he was in for cooking meth. I told him I was in for selling it. He had a lot of old biker stories, and the story of his first arrest still sticks with me.

He was cooking meth in a homemade lab that he'd used many times before, but this time he had some flaky people helping him. One of them knocked over a Bunsen burner and caused a big explosion. The mark I saw on his face was part of the 3rd degree burn that covered the whole side of his body. He went straight from the hospital to jail when he was finally healed enough to travel.

While we were talking that very first time, I was also checking out the cell that was going to be my home for now. It had two metal bunks coming out of the wall; the outside two corners of the bed were supported by chain. Sitting on the bottom bunk, with my back against the wall, I couldn't straighten my legs completely out before touching the other wall. It was so narrow that they had to put the toilet down at the foot of the beds, with the small sink right next to it. They were both made out of stainless steel. A mirror on the wall above the sink was also made out of shiny steel, but it was so scratched up, it was pretty useless. He already had the bottom bunk, so that left me the top. That was OK with me; I didn't really want to see him try to climb up there all the time. His name completely escapes me, so I'll just call him Joe. Joe the biker had been here before, so he knew the routine. I just walked around with him and asked a lot of questions. Well, what walking we could do.

I guess the very first time that I realized I might have a purpose here was when Joe got mail one day. It was the first time he had received any mail at all, so I could tell he was really glad to finally feel that someone out there was thinking about him enough to take the time to write. After about five minutes, he asked me to do him a favor. Favors are not easily agreed to in here because you never know what they may want, but I liked Joe, so I asked what he needed. He asked me if I could read his letter to him. I was floored. I couldn't believe anyone could possibly make it through life being illiterate. Just by the small amount of time I had spent in jail so far, I couldn't even imagine how slowly my time would have passed if I had not had books to crawl into and escape. For the next month or so, time flew by rather quickly because I spent it teaching Joe to read. Now, you can't teach someone how to read in a month, but you can put a pretty good dent in it. And when I finally left that cell, headed to a new place for them to lock me up, at least I knew Joe would continue where we left off now that he was finally past the embarrassment of being illiterate. That embarrassment is what keeps many of the people who can't read from ever taking that first step to start learning. Once you explain to a guy that everyone is constantly learning, including me, learning isn't something to ever be embarrassed about. In fact, it's something to be very proud of.

West Block was a holding pen for all Northern California convicts waiting for placement in other institutions. The institutions are rated for the type of inmates they contain. Level four was where all the baddies go. Pelican Bay is a level four institution. They sent inmates there who attacked guards or killed each other while already here in prison for other convictions. They sent some of the baddest gang-bangers there, anyone they considered any type of real threat to the officers. In Pelican Bay, you have almost no contact with each other. The mail comes in on video, you take one step out of your cell to shower, food is brought to you, and anything else they can think of to completely isolate you and break your spirit. Some of those spirits are pretty tough to affect at all.

So any level of inmate could be here in West Block, from level one to level four. We were in our cells for about twenty-three hours a day, only coming out to walk to breakfast and dinner. While at breakfast, we were given a brown cardboard box with a prepackaged lunch. Sometimes it had two slices of meat, sometimes it had two slices of cheese, but never both. It was another one of those small weird things that I noticed while there, as if they did it on purpose. Actually, after being in there, I KNOW they did it on purpose. They did everything in there after careful calculation. They purposely, openly encouraged racial discrimination. They segregated us as mush as possible, trying to keep that tension high. Separate weight piles, separate areas to eat, everything was segregated. They figured that if we were after one another, we would be less likely to commit acts to the guards. When I heard a few years ago about the prison guards that were getting convicts to fight each other and betting on it, I wasn't surprised at all. That was the mentality in there. We were looked upon as dogs, and just as some enjoy seeing dogs fight to the death, they didn't really see us as much differently and felt we should be treated the same.

During one of the first trips to the chow hall for breakfast, three black guys were arguing right in front of us during the walk there. It had something to do with a dope deal out on the streets, and how two of the guys were really pissed at the other guy. But they were being very quiet about the whole situation. Usually, they made a lot of noise when they argued or fought. I don't know if they did it to try to intimidate you or hoped that the noise would get the guards over quicker to break up the fight.

My cellie whispered over to me, "Even if you are paying attention to them, at least pretend like you aren't. The less you know in here about other people's business, the better off you are. Nobody wants you all up in what they are doing. And you'll see that everyone has some kind of hustle going on in here."

We ate breakfast and got our box lunches on the way out the door. We walked from there back to West Block, three or four wide until we got to the big iron doors that enclose West Block inside. Then, we stopped and waited while they locked the door we just came through, and then unlocked and opened the iron doors in front of us. The three black guys from earlier were in front of us again, except there were about six of them now. It seemed to be five against one. One of the five said something about him getting his, the guy alone said fuck you, and stopped walking in line. The rest of us kept walking, and he fell back behind us in the large group of about 500 guys. We went on in, up the stairs to the third tier, and started walking down the walkway to our cell. About halfway down the tier, we heard shouting come from above us, and just like that, the black guy who was arguing with the other five, came tumbling past us from off of the fourth or fifth tier. He screamed until he hit the cement on the bottom floor, where he went silent. Well, I saw this whole thing unfold, but never expected it to escalate this quickly to someone getting seriously hurt or killed. All I could seem to keep running through my mind was 'Welcome to San Quentin.' I looked around for the guards with the rifles who walked the catwalks on the outside perimeter, but they were nowhere to be found. As I walked toward my cell, I peeked over the edge and saw a few officers forming around the guy, but no one was touching him. I assumed they were waiting for medics to come down from the hospital. I never found out what happened to the guy or if he survived, and at the time, I truly didn't care. It was none of my business

When we got to our cells, I noticed those red painted garbage cans again at the corner of every sniper cop's catwalk. I asked Joe, "Hey, what are the garbage cans for?"

He said, "Well, you see how we are surrounded by concrete? And you see that sign there that says, "no warning shots fired?" That's doesn't mean, no shots fired. It means that they aim at you when they shoot. If they miss, or one of those rifle bullets passes through the body, where do you think that bullet goes? It would ricochet around these walls 'til it found a soft body to settle in. Those garbage cans are full of sand, which stops the bullet from bouncing around. I bet if you went up there and looked closely, the cans probably have a few bullet holes in them."

Well, that was another eye opening realization. I could accidentally get shot at any time. San Quentin has got to be the place that I learned the lesson, "you can't concern yourself with things you have no control over." Otherwise all of these worries would have torn me apart. I had enough to do taking care of myself in there; I couldn't worry about things that might or might not happen.

After about a month in West Block, we were allowed to go to canteen and buy some personal stuff. It was also something different, after a month of doing the same thing each day. We went up to the upper yard and stood in line for about an hour. It was single file lines and we weren't allowed to talk. It was silent up there because you only got this opportunity once a month and no one wanted to lose their privilege and have to go another month without cigarettes or coffee. There were six lanes painted on the asphalt, each of them leading up to a window in the canteen. The area was covered by a roof, so we could even stand there when it was raining. There was a catwalk along the roof edge with an armed guard walking around, watching everything.

A little farther back in line, two rows over, two 'brothers' were arguing about how much one owed the other. They didn't seem to be coming to any type of agreement, so one hit the other. I wasn't really paying attention to the whole thing until the fight broke out. Some others started yelling and things started to get ugly when the officer up on the catwalk shot one of the convicts fighting right in the back. He went down hard, like someone pushed him over. The guard shot another round, which I saw skip off of the ground in a puff of asphalt, before it hit another convict in the thigh. This convict was just in the wrong place at the wrong time. At this point, all of us hit the dirt. You figure, the lower your body is to the ground, the less of a target it is for a stray bullet. After a few minutes, they took us all back to our cells and we had to wait two more days before we could go to canteen. I listened to other conversations, and none of them were about any concern for the convicts shot, but some of them were about how two assholes screwed up our chance to get cigarettes. As I said before, Welcome to San Quentin.

CHAPTER 14
MIDNIGHT ROUNDUP

A few days later they called out my cellies' name and told him to roll up his stuff; he was shipping out. Just like that, I had the cell to myself. Of course, the first thing I did was to move all of my bedding down to the bottom bunk. Too bad I was only down there for a few hours. At about midnight, they came down to my cell and told me to roll up my stuff. I asked them where I was going, but they wouldn't tell me. So I packed what little I had, and followed the two guards out of West Block.

We went through about five different gates, doors, or checkpoints where they had to unlock and relock, with that loud sound of metal against metal. The sound was very loud at midnight, with no other sounds around but us. After we entered the last building, it was obvious that we were in the hospital. They took me up to the second floor, opened up a hospital cell, waited for me to get in it, then locked it up and left. They never really said much to me the whole time, and when they did, it was just to say "I don't know," or "be quiet." I knew why I was there; I just wanted to hear it from someone I so knew it was true.

The room was larger than my last cell, almost twice as big, and the door was a solid piece of metal, rather than iron bars. The door had a little window in it, and a slot that would fit a tray of food. It had a real hospital bed with a real mattress on it. You could even raise the head up so you were sitting up. The toilet and sink were ceramic as well, rather than shiny stainless steel. I had a window that opened to an inaccessible courtyard. Four walls of windows from other hospital rooms all faced each other, and at the bottom was the roof of the first floor building. Three times a day someone brought me a tray of food, but that was it. I had no contact with anyone for the first two or three days. Finally, someone looked into the window of my cell door. It was a 'brother' with cornrows. It was obvious he was a convict. He just stared for a few seconds, then said, "You must me one of the sickies, huh?"

I said, "What the fuck are you talking about?"

He said, "They bring you up here and quarantine you if you got the shit. Then after awhile they'll send you to the gym. The gym is where they put all you AIDS infected faggots. It's so the rest of us in here know who's got it."

Well, here begins one of the endless struggles I've endured since testing positive, feeling the need to clarify my sexuality. I have nothing against gay people; some of my closest friends are gay. But just because I have this disease, a lot of people make assumptions that are wrong. Back then, it was very important to me that others knew how I got this and not just go by assumptions. Now a-days, it's not so important anymore. People are going to think whatever they want about you, and there isn't much you can do about it. I am at the point now where I don't really care who knows; otherwise I never would have been able to write about it.

It really pissed me off that I had to find out why I was in there from some asshole convict rather than from a doctor or nurse. But in there, they had no post-test counseling. I was only in this hospital room for three weeks before being sent down to the gym, but in those three weeks, three people committed suicide. The hospital wasn't a very cheerful place to begin with, so when you end up there because of testing positive, and you get no one to talk to, it's easy to see how someone could kill himself. All of the loneliness and solitude of prison can drive a sane person crazy. Cops are constantly trying to push your buttons, other inmates are checking to see how far they can push the envelope with you, and your own mind is playing games with you just because it is bored and has nothing better to do.

After a few days, locked up in this hospital cell, I was ready for anything new. Each day seemed to take a week to go by, and the only things to look forward to were meals. We got two hot meals a day and a box lunch that came with our breakfast. But in the hospital, it was brought to you; you weren't allowed to go anywhere. They gave each person a pinprick when they first came into the hospital, to test you for tuberculosis, and until the results are recorded, you were quarantined to protect the rest of the prisoners. With no one to talk to, all you could really do was talk to yourself. I had no paper or pencil, so I couldn't write. I had to find some way to spend my time or this isolation was going to really to get to me.

When I looked out the window into the empty, inaccessible courtyard, I started to imagine how long I might be totally alone like this. I opened the window and heard voices. For a little while, I just eavesdropped in on what was being said. After listening for a bit, I realized that the other people were in the hospital for the same reason I was. I started talking to the other window people. Unfortunately, we didn't really have much else to do besides talk. This is where I met my friend, Jimmy. We ran in the same circles but never really met one another. We knew all the same people, and we were even born and raised in the same town in the Midwest.

Jimmy Mason was one of those guys that you couldn't help but like. He had a very quick smile and always made you laugh. He was like a teddy bear, which he had tattooed on his arm to prove the point. He was very quick at lending a hand, no matter what that help might entail. He would give his last penny to a friend in need, which got him screwed over every so often. But it never deterred him, never changed his outlook on people or his desire to be kind.

After I got out of prison, Jimmy got into a drug program and began completing each of the program steps, one at a time. It was nice to see someone else that I was in prison with, trying to make something out of his life. He was great support for me in my attempt to stay clean and sober.

Jimmy was HIV+ and was having frequent medical complications due to his illness. It seemed like each time he managed to fight past an illness, another would sneak up and kick his ass. I believe that all of his medical issues eventually got to him and after five years of sobriety, he went out and got high. He went on a four-day bender that ended with him dying in a bathtub in a seedy motel.

Although his actual cause of death wasn't AIDS, I still felt that he deserved a panel in the National AIDS Quilt. With the help of some very close friends, we spent a lot of time making that panel and reminiscing about Jimmy. I even sewed a stuffed teddy bear to the panel, because that described Jimmy best. I truly miss you, Jimmy. At this point, I've helped others create eight panels for the quilt, not to mention all of the ones that passed without ever having a panel made.

We had a lot of time to talk and reflect back to when we were free. We talked for about three weeks, until they came and took both of us down to the gym to be with the rest of the 'sickies.' It turned out to be good and bad. It was nice to be able to talk with others who were suffering from the same issues, but you were segregated to a separate living quarters. We slept in bunk beds with about 150 other people. The rest of the day consisted of regular day-to-day routines, just like the rest of the prisoners. We went to breakfast with everyone else, worked the same jobs, used the same yard, went to the same school, and saw the same doctors. The only real difference was where we slept at night.

The nurses had to have one of the worst jobs ever. They had to deal with assholes all day long, and most of the assholes weren't convicts. They tried to help us and give us proper medical attention, but they were constantly interrupted and told they couldn't do this and they had to do that. A few of the nurses quit just out of frustration. They weren't allowed to seem like they cared about us and were told to treat us like the animals we deserved to be treated like.

I grew to really care about these nurses and felt sorry for the way the officers treated them. All they could really do was sit back and watch us die. You could see how it was breaking their hearts. With a lot of time on my hands, I spent it with the nurses in the gym, helping them in any way I could. I filed papers, cleaned up for them, and just sat around talking to them, trying to discover why someone would freely put themselves in this kind of situation, just to feel as if they were constantly banging their heads against the wall. I found that it takes a very special type of person to become a nurse, and an even more special type to want to work at a prison.

One day, I went up to the nurses' station, and they were in there whispering and they looked really sad. I asked what was going on and they told me that another inmate had committed suicide up at the hospital. I said, "Another? How many have killed themselves up there?"

One nurse said, "Unfortunately, it happens all too often. Guys are testing positive and being put up in those hospital cells with no one to talk to and no type of post-test counseling." After sitting alone in a cell for a few days, your mind can play games and you can fall into a pretty deep depression. I know this feeling first hand. You just want someone, anyone, to talk to. After hearing this from the nurses, I came up with an idea that I thought might help out.

I asked the nurses if there was any way I could start doing post-test counseling with the inmates. I told them that I could easily find a few other HIV positive inmates willing to help me with this, and we could really do something to stop this suicide problem. The nurses thought it was a wonderful idea, but doubted we could ever get the guards and prison officials to go along with it. I agreed that the hardest part would be getting permission to do it, but after that, it would be smooth sailing. I had a lot of ideas floating around in my head and I couldn't wait to start this endeavor. I felt that it would give me a chance to feel like I was actually contributing to others around me, rather than just wheeling and dealing, like I had been doing for the past five years.

At about this time, my friend Duane and a few other inmates started a lawsuit against San Quentin and Vacaville prisons for improper treatment of inmates and poor medical attention. Actually, I think the lawsuit started before this, but this was the point where things started to get hot for the prisons. A lawyer was coming up twice a week to interview a few prisoners and take statements. He was getting the same story from each one, about the close living quarters, lack of life saving medications, and poor treatment all around when it came to us. We were treated very poorly by the prison guards.

I told him about one time, when going to the hospital to see the dentist, as we walked through the yard heading to the medical building, every time we walked past a group of inmates, the guard would yell out, "Dead man walking." He thought this was very amusing and seemed to make himself laugh every time he said it. The other inmates just seemed to ignore him, but he wasn't saying it for their benefit anyway. It was just a way to entertain himself.

The attorney couldn't believe we were treated in this fashion, but after hearing the same stories over and over again from different inmates, he didn't have a choice. I also told the attorney about the suicides and how some others have died due to lack of medications. I told him about how we needed some sort of counseling and support with this and we were not getting it. He told me that he would see what he could do from his angle with this and he would get back to me. I never heard from the attorney again, but three weeks later, a memo came to the nurses office asking about post-test counseling and what steps would need to be taken to start this and get it in place.

After talking with the nurses, a small group of us wanted to first go up to the hospital just to talk to the guys locked up there. We wanted to give them some books to read and some literature on HIV. Mainly, we just wanted to give them hope, which was something they didn't have at the time. We weren't allowed much time, but the time we had, we made full use of, and at least I can say there were no more suicides.

The nurses also came up with the idea of a prison orientation where a few inmates would give a little speech to every busload of prisoners that came into San Quentin, as soon as they finished with intake in Receiving & Release. They felt that I would be very helpful with this, since I had a story that showed that HIV is contractible even if you aren't gay and never used a needle. So for a few months, I spoke to two to three groups a day, every day, and told them that anyone can get this. I just told them, in their words, how this virus is color and gender blind, it doesn't care who it infects, and that no one is impervious to it. After each speech, before the inmates were taken away to West Block, two or three from each group walked up to me privately and said that they had no idea, and that they felt maybe they should get tested. I took down their names and told the nurses later, who set up semi-private testing. Nothing in San Quentin was completely private. Everyone seemed to know everyone else's business.

After a few months, I began to see some of the people I gave the speech to, now down in the gym with me. I would talk to them, and they would tell me how they would never have even tested if I hadn't talked to them. For a while, I felt like I was really doing something good, helping out and helping others.

But that feeling began to fade after seeing how we were still being treated and segregated just enough to allow the other prisoners to make judgments about us. Then, we were expected to work, eat and live with these other inmates. Most of the inmates didn't truly give a fuck about us and just wished we were dead, but there were some who had real issues with us and didn't want us around. We were treated unfairly by officers, as well as inmates, only because we took a test that I bet some of them would fail as well if they were tested.

I became very disillusioned by it all. I felt that what I was doing might be very helpful on the outside, but inside, I was just asking people to carry the same stigma I was burdened with, and how testing in prison wasn't necessarily a smart move. Maybe waiting until you got out was a more sound way of thinking. Testing in prison just made your life in there harder, and it was already hard enough as it was. I've skipped a lot of the drama in prison, mainly because the fighting and drama aren't what this book is about, but also because I seemed to find a way to stay uninvolved with all this drama. It was easy to spot when some serious shit was about to come down, and I learned quickly how to avoid this and make sure I was somewhere else at the time. We went into lockdown often, mainly because one group was fighting with another group, and I assume that they figured if they locked all of us up for a while, we would forget what we were fighting about. That didn't seem to happen, but at least during the lockdowns, the guards had it quiet and easy for a little while.

They also locked us down right before and after an execution. As though any of us gave a damn that some piece of shit was getting his life karma repaid in full. I remember how there was one guy who was being executed for killing two teenagers just so he could steal their car to use it in a robbery. He drove them out to a deserted place and killed them both, then went back to the car, and ate the McDonald's food they had just bought. This guy was a grade-A piece of shit, and I was amazed by the number of execution protesters that were outside the prison the night he died. Talk about some poorly placed support, particularly when those of us with our own death sentence were completely ignored. I don't think any of us did anything close to what that sick fuck did, but he was the one who was getting all the support. Ironic or just plain stupid, I'm not sure, but completely unfair, for sure.

On the night of the execution, a few of us sat at the end of the gymnasium, near the double doors, staring outside and talking. A few of the lifers (in prison for life with or without possibility for parole) sat around, talking about how they would escape. It was more a game to them, planning all these things that they would never follow through with, but it kept the mind busy and was entertaining to dream. I seemed to get along best with lifers. They were there for good, and had created some kind of normal life for themselves. They didn't get involved in any of the drama and didn't associate with anyone that did, unless they had to. They used to call me a lifer without the sentence. I guess I could have taken that badly, but I didn't. I could see what they were about and they were the only true stable thing about this whole system. They didn't want to screw up whatever they had created for themselves in prison by getting involved with bullshit that doesn't ever really accomplish anything except getting people hurt.

So there came a point when I felt like I wasn't doing what I had planned to do with this HIV education, so I told the nurses that I felt I needed to do something else. They tried to talk me out of it, which I knew they would, but I had already made up my mind. Maybe someday, once I am outside again, I would continue with the HIV education and peer counseling, but for now, I just didn't feel right, talking guys into taking a test, just to be put down into the same situation I was currently in.

But there were other things I could do to absorb my time. I tutored a little in high school and really liked the feeling I got when I saw that people understood what I was trying to explain to them. I could see the understanding in their eyes and it was obvious that they got it. So I went up to the prison school to talk to the teacher there.

She was a very kind lady, I believe her name was Mrs. Wright, but the name isn't important. What was important was the fact that she had absolutely no reason to be there, but she was there anyway just to help the guys learn. She got very little pay and no acknowledgement for all the hard work she did at that school. After meeting her, I knew I could offer her help, so I asked if she needed a teacher's aid. She told me that she was willing to accept any help, as long as I was serious about wanting to help. I assured her that I was, and I started working there the next week.

I worked at the school for about a year, which turned out to be the most fulfilling job I could have found in there. I taught four guys to read, and helped a score of inmates get their GED's and actually gave them half a chance to do something other than drugs when they got out. One of the saddest things I saw in San Quentin was the revolving door policy that they had. Once a prisoner was set free, he was given 90 bucks and a goodbye. Most of the guys went straight to the dope man to spend that money. I saw guys come and go and come again in there. One friend of mine was only out for one day when he tried to cash a stolen check and was arrested and back in San Quentin that day. It just seemed that no one really wanted to stay out. Some looked at it as having to stand in the corner as a kid; it irritated them, but never really did much to stop whatever it was they got in trouble for. Others looked at it as a small vacation, a chance to rest, fatten up, and get clean, so when they did get out, that first hit would get them really high. No matter what the reason, it was very depressing watching the same guys come back again and again. I swore to myself that there was no way I would ever let my friends see me come walking back, head low in shame, just to get razzed by the other guys for being lame enough to get caught again.

You never hear the guys saying that maybe they shouldn't have been doing the same shit all over again. They just hassle each other over the fact that they got caught again.

Beside those seldom times when mail arrived, the only other real highlight of our boring days were when we made up our canteen lists. We would gather together in a group of about four. We were only allowed to draw canteen once per month, so each of us went to canteen on different weeks of the month. We each had a little list of essentials that we needed and whatever was left over to spend after that went to tobacco and coffee, which we split evenly. It was our form of entertainment, sitting around a checklist of available items, figuring out what we wanted, and adding it all up in the end to see how much money was left over to spend. Later in life, I discovered online grocery shopping. I never tried it because it just seemed a little too much like that checklist that we all sat around. I much prefer the personal feeling you get when you walk through a grocery store, pass other shoppers, change your mind about what you want to buy, and flirt with the checkout girl. I got the flirting part from my father, another of his wonderful gifts.

A person can grow accustomed to hearing the loud clanging of the huge brass keys dangling off of the belt of every guard. We actually used the guards' keys much the same way that mice do with the bell around a cats' neck. We could always hear them coming from down the cellblocks, those keys announcing their presence long before we made any visual contact. Long enough to put things away or to stop whatever it was that we were up to.

Gambling was a very good way for me to pass time and make money in prison. I was very careful choosing whom I gambled with. Pinochle is a card game that took me no time to learn, but a long time to master. I had a lot of spare time to practice and when I learned how to play the single player form of the game, I spent many nights playing with those cards in my bunk. After about a year, I felt that I had a very good handle on the game. Pinochle is a four-player game, so I needed a partner, someone who was just as good as I was.

Baggs was the perfect partner. He was older than me and had a lot of prison experience already. They called him Baggs because he wore a colostomy bag at some point in his life, due to being shot. He had a huge scar across his belly, but you could tell that it was thirty or so years old. So were all of his faded tattoos. He looked like a weathered, old biker and he got a lot of respect from the other convicts and guards.

He was an excellent pinochle player, so the two of us together were unbeatable. Over my entire stay, we must have won over four hundred games and lost only four. Plus, Baggs purposely lost one of those games, just to get the other guys to wager more. I was still extremely pissed off at him for throwing the game. My pride made it hard for me to lose, especially when we should have won. I also prided myself on the fact that we never resorted to any type of cheating. We have even played games where we knew that the other guys were cheating. It made the game a lot closer, but in the end, we still ended up beating them. (Once you figure out how they are cheating, it's not too difficult to screw it all up for them.) Pinochle is a very strategic game. Whenever the other team was cheating, it just changed the strategy a bit. It was really amusing when they got angry when we beat them. They figured that they could go plan out another way to cheat, and then come back for more. We earned fifty to a hundred dollars in canteen each month.

Chess was another game that I discovered. There was this fellow, Bicycle Bill. Bill ran around in the same crowds that I did, out on the streets. We hung out a few times out there, so we were fast friends once we saw each other again on the inside. He was a pretty good chess player. He didn't like to sit down while he played, so I would find myself the only one sitting at the table, he stood at the other side of the table. He was a very cocky player and always talked trash while he played. He was one of the weight pile crew, so he was pretty muscular. He never wore a shirt and was completely covered in tattoos. I think that he just liked showing off his muscles and tattoos. I even caught him flexing in the mirror a couple of times.

He would pace back and forth, talking loudly about what a complicated game chess is, while he soundly kicked my ass game after game. It drove me crazy, not only to be beaten in something, but to have my opponent pacing back and forth, flexing his muscles, and talking constant shit.

I made a comment to him one day about the fact that I believe that I can learn almost anything by reading a book. He laughed and wanted to bet me twenty bucks that I couldn't read a book on chess and beat him. The bet was on.

I went to the prison library and checked out three books on how to play chess. They were the only three books available on the subject. I was actually surprised by the fact that they had three to choose from. Two of the books were almost identical in content, so I had two books to read. I told Bill that I wouldn't play him for a week, but I played other people. Once I learned how to watch what my opponent was trying to do while attacking and defending with my pieces, I knew Bill was in trouble.

After a week, Bill was really impatient to play. I think that he missed talking all that nonsense. We set up the chessboard while I jokingly asked him how many moves he wanted to lose in. He said in as few as possible.

I beat him in seven moves, but I told him that it was a trap trick the book taught me, and that once you learn it, no one could ever use it on you. He was mad about losing so quickly, but I told him that it was a trick, and we'd play another real game for the twenty. He was just happy to get another chance, since I had already legitimately won. We played another game while I sat at my side of the table and began to get vocal. He was still shell-shocked from losing the first game. He didn't make much noise at all. That was all right; I made enough noise for the both of us. When I finally beat him for the second time, he knocked his king over and stormed off. It was a tough lesson for him to learn, but he had to learn it. He never talked shit and got loud during any more of our chess matches, which was a pleasant change for the better. After about three more weeks of me constantly beating him, I told him that I had read somewhere that continual pacing can cause lack of concentration. I completely made it up, but he considered it for a moment before concluding that it must be that pacing that was causing the problem. He sat during every single game that we played after that. Unfortunately, by the time that I had him groomed to be the perfect chess opponent, he wasn't really any competition anymore and I got tired of winning every game. I'm sure that he was growing just as tired of losing. Every now and then, he would challenge me to a game, but not like before. One week after I beat Bill for the first time, I saw him reading one of the chess books that I had returned to the library. It bothered him that he couldn't learn to play as I did from a book, but that's always been easy for me. Books have always had the ability to teach me. I get a lot out of a book. Maybe, that's why I'm writing one!

CHAPTER 15
FREEDOM AT LAST!! SORT OF

When a prisoner has less than six months left on his sentence, he can apply for a Work Furlough Program. Work Furlough sends you to a dormitory style living program outside of the prison walls. You could leave during the day to go to work, but you had to return to the house at night. There was constant drug testing and close supervision. One out of every three prisoners that gets sent to Work Furlough either runs away once he is there or gets sent back to prison for violating one of the house rules. Usually, that included getting high and giving a dirty drug test. To this day, I still can't fathom the logic in running away with less than six months left on your sentence. Once they get caught, they will have an added charge of escape added to their sentence, which means more time.

Here's a funny fact that I learned in prison. Almost every escapee is caught within blocks of where he was originally busted. Once they have escaped, the only thing they know is what they left behind. Instinctively, they go back to the only world they know.

Most convicts look at Work Furlough only as a way to get out of prison. It's a change of pace from the every day life of prison. They get a few more freedoms as well as finally setting foot outside of the prison walls. It was a chance to see friends, eat good food for a change, and to feel like a human being again.

I didn't look at Work Furlough as a way out. It was a chance to get a job, save a little money for a very expensive and tiny apartment in San Francisco, and figure a way to start a life outside my drug world. Work Furlough would give me a chance to step out into the free world, without having to dive in head first with no life jacket on. I didn't have to worry about a roof over my head or where I was going to eat. I only had to go to work every day and get used to having a job. Three years of steady prison life had adapted me to working every day. Work in prison was a way to make time go by a little quicker and it took my mind off of my problems. I looked forward to going to work in prison; it was usually my best form of entertainment except reading a book.

Eight or nine months before my projected release date, I began starting the paperwork to apply for Work Furlough. In order to be eligible for Work Furlough, they looked at the reason that you there in the first place, whether you got in trouble while incarcerated, and what you did with your time while you were there. I knew that with my HIV orientation and teaching at the school, my record looked really good.

They post on a wall a list of people scheduled for the bus to Work Furlough.

Two friends of mine and I were waiting to see if our names were on it. Their names were both listed, but my name was nowhere to be found. I must have searched it three times and it was a list of only twenty-four inmates.

I walked up to one of the few prison guards that I got along with and asked him if he knew why I wasn't on the list. He said that he had no idea and he would check for me. Later that day, he came over to the Pinochle tables and told me that the reason I was turned down was my HIV+ status. Work Furlough said that they didn't have any medical facilities to house HIV+ inmates. I was the first HIV+ person to apply for the program and they didn't really know how to handle that.

I knew that I now had a fight on my hands and I was going to bitch and complain until they got so sick of me that they were going to send me to Work Furlough or they were going to have to release me early to shut me the hell up. I wrote letters of complaint up the chain of command every day, sometimes two a day, turning one in to the day guard on duty and the other one to the night guard.

I complained to the nursing staff, which did everything in their power to help me. Unfortunately, their power was non-existent in this case. It drove me crazy. I was perfectly healthy, on no medications, and discovered this disease in me at the earliest possible stage. I felt that I was no different than anyone else. I needed Work Furlough in order to get a start on life and I deserved it for all of the work I contributed while I was in prison.

I called my Dad and told him what was going on and how no one seemed to want to listen to my complaints. I didn't really think he could do anything about it, but he was a good ear to talk to. About four days after I talked to my Dad, I was called into the Captain's Office. They told me that they were going to make a special exception in my case and send me to Work Furlough. I had to sign an agreement that I would return to the prison if I got sick. No problem, I had no intention of getting sick.

They drove me to Work Furlough program in a van, all by myself. Two and a half months late, I finally arrived at Work Furlough with three and a half months left to go in my sentence. I never did find out if my Dad had anything to do with it but the timing was very coincidental. He's always seemed like a knight in shining armor, so maybe he had something to so with it. Who knows?

A month into the Work Furlough Program, I went to visit a Friend's Outside office. They helped people on the outside get in contact with loved ones on the inside. They also helped men and women on the inside acquire things like books, toiletries, and arts and crafts. They were very resourceful, so I went to see them. Maybe they could offer me some advice.

They told me about a Union Electrician Program that was testing for entrance. They only held testing once a year, sometimes not even that often. They gave me a little pamphlet of info on the testing to take with me. This sounded like a very interesting lead and I was going to follow up on it.

I showed the pamphlet to the counselor at the Work Furlough Program, stressing the point that I only had this one chance to take these tests. She said it sounded like an excellent opportunity for me, but that it had to be cleared by the powers above. That's the usual story with prison life. This was still prison, no matter how many freedoms they gave you or how free you felt.

I was summoned to her office a few days later. She said that her superiors informed her that since the testing site was in another county, I wasn't allowed to go. One condition of my parole was that I had to stay in San Francisco County. It was also a rule of the Work Furlough house.

Well, I did what any person like me would do in a situation like that, I bawled like a baby. O.K., I didn't cry but I threw a fit. I made it very apparent exactly how I felt about the subject. I stormed out of her office pretty pissed off. I stewed on it all night in my bunk, trying to think of a way to change their minds.

The next morning, breakfast came and went, but I still sat on my bunk. Checkout time also came and went. Checkout time is when we sign out for the day with the location of where we plan to be. After all of the other guys had left, the officer in charge came over to my bed and asked if I was sick. I told him no. He wanted to know why I wasn't checking out. I told him that I wanted to go back to San Quentin. I wasn't happy with the amount of trouble I went through just to get into this program. When I wanted to try to do something constructive with my life, they told me that some stupid technicality was going to keep me from taking my first step forward to becoming something other than a really good drug dealer. Out of the fifty inmates that were in the Work Furlough Program with me, ten of us were actually out trying to find work and taking this whole situation seriously. The other forty were out with friends or girlfriends and not looking for work at all. I knew that I had worked harder in this program than anyone else. I took this opportunity very seriously. If they weren't going to allow me to take it seriously, then I didn't want to be there.

They didn't know what to do with me and my counselor wasn't coming in that day. So they just let me sit there and sit there I did. Other guys brought me food; they thought the whole sit down strike was very amusing. At least I had someone on my side.

The next morning, as soon as my counselor walked in the front door, I saw the guards talking to her. She came over to my bunk with her briefcase still in her hand, no chance to even get to her desk yet. She could see immediately how upset I was. I explained to her that my mind was made up and I wanted to go back to San Quentin to finish my time there. Less trouble, less stress, and fewer headaches sounded very appealing to me right then. She told me to wait there and she was going to take her briefcase to her desk, unpack, and see what other catastrophes happened while she was away for a day. Like I planned to go anywhere? I was on a sit my ass on my bunk strike and I was prepared for battle.

The employees that acted as security and oversaw the day to day living, although they were hired free people not officers, were called guards by all of us. Whether they had a uniform on or not made no difference at all, a guard is a guard. One of these 'guards' walked up to my bunk and said that the counselor wanted to see me in her office.

I went up to her office fully expecting to be told that a van was on the way to take me on the short ride back to San Quentin and I needed to get my belongings together. When I got there, she told me to close the door and sit down. She explained that for me to leave the county was against the rules and regulations. She said, that on the day of the tests, I was to checkout in the morning and in the spot for destination, I was to write in her name. She would explain to the guards that I offered to help her out by running a few errands for her. The guards would be happy that the problem was alleviated, and it didn't really matter to them how it was fixed. She also stressed that this was a personal favor she was doing for me and that she was taking a risk. If I got into trouble or broke the law over in Alameda County, there was nothing she could do for me. She said that this was between her and me and I wasn't to tell anyone about it. She said this was a special circumstance. I told her that I wouldn't say anything to anyone; I only wanted the opportunity to take these tests. She also said that if I screwed up, she would personally drive to San Quentin to kick my ass. From her posture and the dead stare that she gave me, I could tell that she meant every word of it. I never told anyone except my wife until now; I figure I kept the promise long enough.

I took the Bay Area Rapid Transit or BART to get to the testing site. BART is an expansive light rail system that covers four counties in the Bay Area (SF, Alameda, San Jose, and Contra Costa Counties.) It runs through a tube laid across the ocean floor, spanning the SF Bay, from San Francisco to Oakland. I love riding the BART; it's comfortable and relaxing. If you ever get a chance to ride it, it's the best way to get around in the Bay Area.

I aced all three of the tests, scoring the highest score there for both of the math tests and in the top three in the spatial relations test. Even with scores so high, they didn't call me again for two years. After discovering how the union chooses its apprentices, I'm surprised that I made it at all. Unions give the first open seats in the apprenticeship to relatives and personal friends of electricians already in the union. If there are any open seats after that, they go to their waiting list of applicants.

I had to go through an oral interview with an old, weathered electrician who looked tired. He asked all sorts of questions about why I wanted to be an electrician and what I planned to do with the education that they were providing. I seemed to impress him with my answers; he went from frowning at the initial handshake to smiling by the end of the interview. His hand felt like burlap when I shook it and his grip was like a vice.

After a moment of silence, he said, "Are you sure that this is what you want to do for the rest of your life? This trade is hard on the body; many guys end up with bad backs and bum knees."

I said, "Yes, this is definitely what I want and I hope you'll allow me the chance."

He laughed and said, "O.K., one more thing. Hold up your hands." I held my hands out in front of me with my fingers spread apart. Now, he said, " Look at 'em." I looked down and saw my hands. Well, this is easy. He said, "No, I mean really look at 'em. Turn 'em over a couple times and really study them." Then, I was really looking at my hands, turning them over a couple times, but they still just seemed like a bunch of fingers and two thumbs.

As he lifted two gnarled tree trunks for hands, cracked and weathered from years of hard labor, he said, "You'd better remember what those hands look like now because that's the prettiest you'll ever see 'em."

A good lesson learned that day. I have worn work gloves every day at work, so after ten years of construction, I still have normal hands, unlike some guys in the trade, whose hands feel like they are permanently wearing gloves.

I left the interview with a good feeling about the entire process I went through with the apprenticeship. Unfortunately, they didn't contact me for almost three years with any information about starting classes or getting work in the electrical field. A year after that, I finally started my first class in the apprenticeship and things started to fall into place for the best possible career that I could have chosen for myself. Until that life changing phone call, I had to find other forms of employment to keep my mind occupied and to pay my bills.

CHAPTER 16
LIFE GOES ON

I have discovered over the course of my life that I personally need a certain type of job to keep me entertained enough to make it through the day. I don't mind a hard, physical day at work, as long as I am doing different tasks throughout the day. Boredom is my worst enemy at work. Whenever I have nothing to do, the day seems to drag by in slow motion. I get the same slow motion feeling whenever I am doing any routine, repetitious task. After the fourth or fifth time, it grows boring. A good day of work for me is when I look at the clock in the morning to start the day and the next thing I know, it's lunchtime. The rest of the day flies by just as fast when I keep busy. Unfortunately, with no college education and a felony record hanging over my head, not many employers seemed interested in giving an ex-con a job. I felt as if I had a tattoo on my forehead that said "DO NOT HIRE." I was always very upfront about my past because lying on your job application is cause for an immediate dismissal. I didn't want a job where I worried every day whether or not this would be the day that they found out about my record. Parole Officers also have a habit of popping in at work on parolees to make sure that they really were at work. That would have been hard to explain to my employer.

I looked for a job that would take advantage of my knowledge of the San Francisco streets. I lived on them for so long, I knew the layout of almost the entire city. In the next four years, while I waited for that phone call about the apprenticeship, I managed to find two different jobs. The first job was easy to get and the second job was even better than the first.

I went back to the Work Furlough Program that night exhilarated from my day with the union. I wanted to tell everyone about my experiences and how these experiences had brought me hope. That's something I hadn't had for a very long time. However, I promised my counselor that I wouldn't say anything about it so I kept my mouth shut. Instead, I walked around the building asking others how their day was and about their luck job hunting.

There wasn't much luck in the search for work for them because most of them talked about what they managed to get away with during the day, not about attempting to find a job. One guy told me that they were hiring at a bike messenger service and they didn't ask you about your past record. I asked him where they were located and decided to go there the next morning. Maybe I would have two great days in a row? I sure could use them.

The next morning, I checked out of the program, writing the address of the delivery service as my destination. Three blocks away from the Work Furlough

Program is the local headquarters of a popular motorcycle club in the Bay Area. A couple of the white guys in the program stopped by there before hopping the bus to the downtown area. They knew guys there at the clubhouse that had also been in prison, so they went by the clubhouse to say "Hi" or 'whatever else.' The 'whatever else' was absolutely none of my business, so I kept it that way. I stopped in every now and then, just to see if anyone I knew was there. I went there since it was on the way to the bus stop.

While we were talking, I said, "I'm going down to apply for a job as a bike messenger."

One of the guys said, " I wonder if you can use a motorcycle? We could find you one to use."

I laughed and replied, "Yeah, right! Ripping up and down SF city streets all day long on the loudest motorcycle in the world. I don't think they'd be too happy about that."

It was very nice of them to offer the help. I could tell that it was out of true kindness and a desire to help. But, who wants to owe anything to a biker?

Applying to be a bike messenger was quick and simple. I had to fill out a couple of forms that didn't ask me any personal questions about me besides my address and driver's license number. I put down the address of the Work Furlough Program. I was hired in thirty minutes and told to come back the next day to start. I was asked if I wanted to ride a bicycle or moped. I remembered pedaling up those hills all tweaked out of my mind and didn't want to try to battle those hills all day long, clean and sober, if I didn't have to. I took the obvious choice and picked the moped.

When I arrived at the shop the next day, they handed me a moped with pedals. I knew immediately that it was going to be a long day. I quickly learned why being a messenger is one of the most dangerous professions you can choose.

As well as riding a beat up, two-wheeled bicycle with a small engine, I had a thousand obstacles to dodge. It became a game, getting from one office building all the way across town to another. I timed myself to see how fast I could get from point A to point B without hitting anything or killing myself. There were close calls every day and bumps and scrapes on me and other objects, but they went unreported for the most part.

Working as a messenger kept me busy and out of trouble, mainly because I was too exhausted after a long day of work to do anything but sleep until the next day. Eventually, I was released from the Work Furlough Program and moved in with my soon-to-be wife and her father. Life began to feel normal for the first time. Going to work every day, coming home to have dinner with a family, and every other little thing that I did to live was new and felt right. I knew from the very beginning that this was what I wanted.

The longer a person is a messenger, the better the odds of having an accident. Eventually, one of those close calls is going to go the wrong way. I made it more than two years before my close call went in a sour direction. Until that moment, I think I felt invincible and that I would never get hit.

I was riding down a three-lane, one-way street in the downtown, business area of the city. I was in the left lane and I really liked this street because, at the slow pace of my moped, the lights were timed all the way down the street. If you drove the street at 35, like a car would, you would have to brake at every light for a moment. A woman driving in the far right lane decided to turn left at the next intersection and drove right into me. She was very apologetic and said that she didn't see me. I didn't mention to her the fact that I was wearing a huge, fluorescent orange helmet. I just wanted to sit down and collect myself. While I was hobbling out of the street and over to the sidewalk, I called my dispatcher with the radio that I had strapped into a harness across my chest.

I radioed, "Tristin, I just got hit by a car."

She immediately responded, "Oh no, honey, are you O.K.? Should I call an ambulance?"

I said, "No, no ambulance. My bike needs to be picked up and I need to go see a doctor because I think I broke my foot."

After a few seconds, she said, "O.K., help is on the way. Stay put and relax, you are gonna be fine."

I gave her my location and told her where, exactly, on the corner I was located. Within minutes, twenty bike messengers showed up, some from other messenger companies. Messengers heard that one of their own was injured and they stopped whatever it was they were doing to go see if they could offer any help. Some of them piled their messenger bags up behind me so I could sit up comfortably, while others collected information from the woman who had hit me.

Watching the way everyone performed their tasks, I saw that this obviously wasn't the first or last time any one of these road warriors was going to have to go through this exact same drill for another messenger in need. If more people acted this way, the world would be a better place.

That was all of the incentive I needed to decide to make a career change. I wanted to find a job that took advantage of my knowledge of the city streets, but yet, I want some metal wrapped around me for protection. So of course, I chose one of the other most dangerous professions in the city and became a taxicab driver. I had a cast on my foot and nothing better to do with my time, so I completed every one of the intake steps while I waited to have the cast removed before I could start working.

Driving a taxicab in San Francisco was a very interesting and entertainming job. I met all sorts of unique people and everyone had a story. When someone climbs into the back of a cab, they seem to talk about anything. It's almost like his private confessional booth, I guess. They figure that they will never see you again, so they can tell you things that they wouldn't tell most people in their lives. I seem to have a way to get people to talk; I always have. Whenever people climbed into the back of my cab, they loosened up. It may also have had something to do with the fact that I was picking a majority of them up to take them home after a long night of drinking and partying. Let's just say, everything that you see on that HBO show, "Taxicab Confessions," is true; I can attest to that.

I asked a few of the veteran cab drivers for a few tips on how to be a better cab driver. They gave me some excellent advice. They said that the secret to making money as a cab driver is to keep your customer talking. The more at home they feel, the bigger the tip in the end. If you can keep your fare talking through the entire ride, then you've done your job. They also told me to learn the city. As well as memorizing the streets, learn a bit of history for each area you travel through. Customers, tourists especially, but local people as well, appreciate it when you have an interesting story or two about San Francisco.

Cab driving was a great job and I met a lot of very nice people, but I was ready to start the apprenticeship. When that phone call finally came, I was ready and willing to start work immediately. Although being an electrician is the best job I've ever had, cab driving was the second best.

This has to be the hardest chapter to write. How do you end a life story, when there is still life yet to live? This seems like the best stopping point. Beyond this, my life has balanced out, mainly due to having a child.

I can still remember what it was like on the streets and in San Quentin, memories like that can never be forgotten. Once in a while, when I wake up in the morning, I am not sure if this is all a dream and I'm still in prison or if I actually made it through the whole ordeal and survived, unlike many of my old friends. I can't really wait until the end of the story to write it because I won't be around by then. Maybe I'll write a second story, to explain what has happened since, but I think this story has come to an end. I was able to put down on paper many of these memories, while at the same time, almost reliving them.

Life hasn't been perfect since becoming an electrician and beginning a new career. I have had my ups and downs, just like anyone else in life. I take each day like it's a whole new adventure. I've had a few health issues and medications are a necessary evil in my life, but on the whole, life is good. I'm still alive and kicking and I feel healthy most of the time. I'm content to accept that and just deal with the bad days, one day at a time.

So you see, even after years of shit and a downward spiral into darkness, even the worst of us can actually make it through to the other side and change. Changing was the easy part, I just had to keep reminding myself that I was needed more out here than I was inside, back in prison. So there is really no moral to this story; just the fact that I made it through and I'm still alive to talk about it is an accomplishment in its own and for that I'm grateful. Now I have a baby girl that is my everything. I can't ever see me going back in the day again because now I have way too much to lose. Everything in life is finally going well for me. I don't want to even rock the boat. I'm off parole, have a great job, and I'm still strong and healthy. I never had anything in life go for me before, so this is a new experience, but an experience I grew to like instantly. I just wish I hadn't had to learn it the hard way, but sometimes, that's the only way you can learn at all.

The End